A Conversation with Ambassador
Richard T. McCormack

A Conversation with Ambassador Richard T. McCormack

Interview by Charles Stuart Kennedy
Initial Session: January 2, 2002

Diplomatic Oral History Series
Association for Diplomatic Studies and Training

Richard T. McCormack

To order additional copies of this book, contact:
Xlibris Corporation
1-888-795-4274
www.Xlibris.com
Orders@Xlibris.com
104725

CONTENTS

Bromley Smith
Columbia; Drug Problems

Under Secretary of State for Economic Affairs—1989-1991
Political Appointee Selection Process
Executive Office Organization
Principal G-7 Economic Summit Coordinator
James Baker
Japan Trade Issues
Revolving Door
European Union
Global Trade in Agriculture
Agriculture Trade Subsidies
U.S. Labor Mobility
The Euro
Houston Economic Summit
Paris Economic Summit
Special Drawing Rights
Soviets
European Bank for Reconstruction Development
U.S. Policy Making Process
President George H.W. Bush
Bob Zoellick
Sudan Famine Relief Program
Israeli Economy
Japanese Finances

Woodrow Wilson Center
Private Sector Consulting
Member of Delegations to Foreign Ministers
Center for Strategic and International Studies (CSIS)
Merrill Lynch

Partial List of Papers Authored by Ambassador McCormack

Dick McCormack at ease in Bradford, Pennsylvania, where it all began.

Richard McCormack (first from the left) with President Nixon and the Ash Council at San Clemente, reviewing the Council's proposed plan to strengthen the White House structure and the broader office of the President. August 1969.

Photo Credit: Nixon Presidential Library and Museum

Ambassador and Karen McCormack with the President and Mrs. Reagan at the White House, July, 1986.

Photo Credit: Ronald Reagan Presidential Foundation and Library

President George HW Bush, and his G-7 economic summit Sherpa, Richard McCormack and Treasury aide, David Mulford, on the roof of the Arc de la Defense in Paris, July 14, 1989, after a successful negotiation.

Photo Credit: George Bush Presidential Library and Museum

To family, friends, and former colleagues who made this journey possible and incredibly rich and enjoyable.

FOREWORD

The ADST Diplomatic Oral History Series

For 235 years extraordinary diplomats have served the United States at home and abroad with courage and dedication. Yet their accomplishments in promoting and protecting American interests usually remain little known to their compatriots. The Association for Diplomatic Studies and Training (ADST) created the Diplomatic Oral History Series to help fill this void by publishing in book form selected transcripts of interviews from its Foreign Affairs Oral History Collection.

The text contained herein acquaints readers with the distinguished career of the Honorable Richard McCormack and his extensive experience in international affairs. We are proud to make his interview available through the Diplomatic Oral History Series.

ADST (www.adst.org) is an independent nonprofit organization founded in 1986 and committed to supporting training of foreign affairs personnel at the State Department's Foreign Service Institute and advancing knowledge of American diplomacy. It sponsors books on diplomacy through its Memoirs and Occasional Papers Series and, jointly with DACOR (an organization of foreign affairs professionals), the Diplomats and Diplomacy Series. In addition to posting oral histories under "Frontline Diplomacy" on the website of the Library of Congress, ADST manages an instructional website at www.usdiplomacy.org.

Kenneth L. Brown
President, ADST

FROM BRADFORD, PA TO SWITZERLAND

Q: When and where were you born?

McCORMACK: I was born in Bradford, Pennsylvania, an oil town in the northern part of the state where my family had been living since the middle of the 19th century.

Q: In what year were you born?

McCORMACK: 1941.

Q: So your family was from that area?

McCORMACK: Yes. My father worked with Dresser Industries, and my mother was from one of the old pioneering oil families in the region.

Q: Now, your father McCormack, was he Irish or Scottish?

McCORMACK: My grandfather, Michael Jennings McCormack, was of Irish origin. His mother was of English heritage.

Q: Do you know when they came over?

McCORMACK: Sometime in the middle of the 19th century.

Q: How about your mother's side?

McCORMACK: Some of them came during William Penn's time; other branches came later in the 18th and 19th centuries.

Q: Oh boy! They weren't Quakers though?

McCORMACK: No. As far as we know, her family was a mixture of English, Scottish, and German.

Q: What about your father? What sort of education did he have?

McCORMACK: A high school education. He was a self-educated man, with a formidable intellect and wide interests.

Q: And your mother?

McCORMACK: After graduating from high school in Bradford, PA, she attended a school in Rochester, NY.

Q: Well then, any brothers or sisters?

McCORMACK: I had one brother who died recently. He was a supervisor at a large business in Bradford—a very bright man and immensely kind.

Q: Did you grow up in Bradford?

McCORMACK: Yes.

Q: Talk about Bradford a bit. What was it like in the '40s and '50s?

McCORMACK: Bradford was a wealthy town. In fact, on a per capita basis, it was supposedly the third wealthiest city in the country when I was growing up. This five-mile by five-mile area produced two billion pre-inflationary dollars worth of oil by the early 1970's. Some of it sold for fifty cents a barrel, and some of it for OPEC prices.

The good thing was that the money was spread throughout the community. There were originally many medium-sized farmers who became oil producers, which is what some of my ancestors were. One big surge of oil production began in the 1870s with natural production. Then in the 1920s, they discovered water flooding, and another third of the oil was extracted over the next thirty years. So, you had two shots of wealth that came into that community during different generations. The second infusion of wealth came after many families had become better educated.

There were about 17,000 people in Bradford at the height of the prosperity. The town was surrounded by mountains and trees, with the Allegheny River flowing a few miles away—just an idyllic place for a boy to grow up.

They had outstanding teachers in the local school system. Children were rarely sent away to school. Most bright youngsters stayed in Bradford and received a superb college prep education.

Q: In elementary school, can you think of any teachers that particularly inspired you or turned you off?

McCORMACK: Yes. When I was asked to address the graduating high school class in 1975 I mentioned a whole list of these people, such as Miss Garnet Bradley in the first grade who took all my initial "C's" and "D's" and turned them into "A's" by the year's end.

Q: In one year?

McCORMACK: In one year. There were teachers like Bill Olson, who took a shy, stuttering sophomore and turned him into a prize-winning extemporaneous speaker in the Western Pennsylvania region. Every night for months he asked me to come in after school and practice. I was so shy when he started that I would flush just standing in front of the room. But night after night he pressed on. I owe him an enormous debt.

Then there were history teachers such as Harriet Titus and several outstanding English teachers and many others, all tremendously dedicated people, who cared about us and who worked with us when we were having difficult years. Because of the lack of other professional opportunities, many intelligent women went into teaching. They were highly dedicated people. We benefited tremendously from them.

When I was in high school, my father suggested that maybe the Foreign Service would be an interesting career for me. He wrote to the State Department for a little pamphlet that described careers in the Foreign

Service. Eventually, I decided to go to Georgetown and take a closer look at Washington, D.C.

Q: Go back. Were there things you were particularly interested in? I am thinking about reading or sports or something like that.

McCORMACK: Yes. I was very interested in history and in current affairs. I used to read *Newsweek* every week from cover to cover.

Q: Where did you get your news in Bradford?

McCORMACK: From *Newsweek* basically, or the odd *New York Times,* and in discussions with my father, who was extremely interested in global affairs, and with my friends in our champion debating society.

Q: Can you think of any sort of books that particularly impressed you?

McCORMACK: As a child I spent much of my time in the local public library. I read all of Churchill's books on the Second World War, which of course were fascinating to me. There was one book, *The American Past,* which I often read in my grandmother's house. It was a book that covered American history from colonial time to 1945.

There were few children's books in my widowed grandmother's house, where I spent a lot of time as a child. I must have read that book fifteen times as a boy, to the point where it became a part of me. In fact, I still have the book and I read it to my own young children. It is a great big thick volume with pictures and articles about America from its earliest roots to 1945.

Q: What about the area around Bradford? During the French and Indian War, was this sort of an historical area?

McCORMACK: Our family had Walter ancestors killed in the French and Indian War further south in Fulton County. But the area in McKean County surrounding Bradford was one of the last settled parts of the east. Some of our people came into this almost pristine valley in the 1830's. Earlier George Washington had signed a treaty with the Seneca Chief,

Cornplanter. Thus the area adjacent to our county was a Seneca Indian reservation.

My father used to invite a Native American family to have Thanksgiving dinner with us. Mr. Barnie Lauer was a widower, and he had a son my age. He worked for my father, and my father was very fond of him. He had lost one arm in a farming accident.

The high altitude often caused the frost to come early in the fall. It was not unusual to have snow in May. The soil was mostly thin and acidic in that area. So it wasn't a natural farming region. My ancestors cut the white pine trees on their hill farm, built rafts of them, floated them, loaded with honey and wool, and sent them down the Allegheny River during the spring floods. Our family discovered oil under that hill in 1872.

Q: I take it there was no tie to what I call John O'Hara country, which was the coal mining belt?

McCORMACK: No, none. Bradford was the oil area, the heart of the Pennsylvania oil fields. Thus, there was for decades a lot of capital and talent in the community. Piper Aircraft started there. Zippo lighters, Case cutlery, Kendall oil, etc., all began in this little community. Dresser Industries had roots there and went on to become a giant corporation. There was a core of educated, intelligent, and sophisticated people because of family ties and the opportunities that were available.

Bradford had a remarkable spirit. The town was, of course, a tiny place but thought of itself then as a regional giant. The town had its own airport, country clubs, and a first-class hospital. The football teams were often excellent. The debating societies won many regional tournaments in those years.

Q: Where did your family fall politically, or did it?

McCORMACK: My father's Irish family was predominantly Democratic. My mother's family was Republican.

Q: Did you have debates at the dinner table?

McCORMACK: Only gentle ones. My father later became a Republican. This area was so overwhelmingly Republican that, if you wanted to have any influence on who your local public servants were, you had to vote in the Republican primary. My father always liked Eisenhower, the president at the time.

Prior to Eisenhower, he had been in favor of Roosevelt since the Depression also impacted Bradford, though less severely than in many other parts of the nation. He was also one of the local leaders who opposed the Ku Klux Klan, which briefly surfaced in the region in the 1920's.

Q: While you were in high school, you were on the debating team in high school. Any other activities?

McCORMACK: I was on the student council and in the honor society. I was a good long—distance runner but not very good at most sports. I was nearsighted, extremely thin, and ill-coordinated. I never lost a wrestling match, however, and I became a fair boxer. I also loved to hunt, fish, and hike in the mountains.

Q: While you were living there, up to the time when you were 18, around 1959 or so in high school, did world affairs intrude at all?

McCORMACK: Yes. You will remember this was the time when we were performing drills and hiding under our desks periodically because of the nuclear threat. At one time there was a great smoke cloud that came over our area for an entire afternoon, which we later heard was either a vast distant forest fire or a civil defense exercise. People were concerned about the possibility that there could be a nuclear conflict.

We didn't spend our days dwelling on this, but it was a reality that we were all aware of. My father, however, one day took me aside and said to me, "Don't worry about the Soviet Union launching a nuclear war. You need to remember that many of the people in that country are like us. They are fathers, uncles, and grandfathers. They know that if there were a nuclear conflict their own families would be incinerated. They are not going to want this to happen. Never allow yourself to demonize all the people on the other side. Most are, in fact, like us—not the top political leadership, of course, because we have a very different system. But they are not fools."

Q: Did you have exchange students? Were you in touch with people coming from outside the country?

McCORMACK: There were one or two in Bradford, but I had little contact with them. There was a civic lecture program to bring in distinguished speakers occasionally, as well as a civic music program. They also had wonderful golfing, horseback riding, grouse shooting, trout fishing, and miles of empty woodlands to walk through.

Q: How did they pry you loose?

McCORMACK: Jack Murphy was president and chairman of Dresser Industries until recently. He came from Olean, NY, which was a similar small oil-based city near the Allegheny River, a few miles from Bradford. He once commented to me at a dinner that we grew up in a kind of paradise but didn't realize it at the time.

I was blessed with a wonderful grandmother. Mina Walter Fox was widowed and ran the family oil lease. She was a strong, intelligent, and generous soul who had an integrity that never stopped. She had lost her beloved husband in 1929 and a favorite son, Tom Fox, a fighter pilot in the Second World War. I came along about that time and she took a keen interest in me.

My grandmother provided me with an educational trust fund, which made it possible for me to attend Georgetown University and to continue my graduate studies to a PhD. level in Switzerland. She was my pal. We spent a lot of time together when I was growing up in Bradford. She had been a teacher prior to marrying my grandfather. She was considered a handsome woman with a great natural dignity.

Q: Coming from a family which was half Irish, did you grow up as a Catholic?

McCORMACK: My mother's family was Protestant and my father's family was Catholic. We were raised as Catholics and my mother later became a Catholic. There was never any religious tension in the families. My maternal grandfather, Thomas Fox, earlier helped raise the funds to build the Methodist church in the Derrick City Valley near Bradford. No one ever spoke ill of another person's religion in the family.

Q: It is interesting because you are coming out of a period when people were not overly tolerant. Both sides tended to demean the other. I mean there were real divisions that these days seem so . . .

McCORMACK: Prior to 1960 there was very little religious interaction in our broader community. In retrospect, that was the regrettable thing in the area, as in much of America. Jews were not permitted to join the country club. There was very little social interaction between the various religious groups within our town.

When I went back to Bradford about three years ago, I stopped in at St. Bernard's Catholic Church on Good Friday to spend a quiet time. I was astonished to see in the pulpit at 12:00 o'clock the Baptist preacher, who spoke for about 15 minutes. Then everybody got up and went to the Baptist church, where the Catholic priest spoke, from there to the Episcopal church, and from there to the EUB church. They went all around the town with a procession of about 300 people, each hearing 15-minute presentations at the various churches.

My wife, Karen Hagstrom, comes from nearby Port Allegany, a similar but smaller community. Her mother was a pillar in the local Republican Party. When I was visiting this town one summer, I noticed that the summer bible school for all the town's children was being held at the Catholic Church. This would have been unthinkable when I was a boy. There have been some not-so-wonderful changes that have happened in America during the last 30 years, but one of the good things is that these artificial religious and social divisions have melted away. There is a much greater degree of tolerance now.

Q: I just two weeks ago saw "South Pacific," in which the plot essentially revolves around intolerance between Polynesians and Americans. I had to explain the movie to my granddaughter because the plot seemed so inexplicable.

McCORMACK: Well, as I noted earlier, that was the not so good thing about America in the 1950s. Whole professions were ethnically Balkanized.

I later wrote my PhD dissertation partly on the effects of racism in colonial Kenya and the harm this caused. Our part of Pennsylvania was never much infected by the racial dimension of things.

Q: I notice you didn't go to a Catholic school.

McCORMACK: Georgetown was a Catholic school.

Q: No, but I mean before that.

McCORMACK: No, I did not. I went to public schools. My father had gone to the public schools, and my father was a committed Catholic and his father was a Catholic. But they felt their children should be exposed to and be part of the broader American society. This was a view that probably came from the family's McCormack/Jennings mixed Irish-Anglo roots.

Within our family no one spoke ill of other religions, and anti-Semitism was deplored. Bigotry on the part of Protestants toward Catholics was deplored. Bigotry of Catholics toward Protestants was deplored.

Q: You were at Georgetown from when, '59 to . . .

McCORMACK: '63.

Q: '63. What was Georgetown University like then?

McCORMACK: It was a university in transition, as the Catholic Church as a whole was in transition. It was the Vatican Council period. It was going from a time when there were many certitudes that later became questions. Georgetown today is a far better university than when I was studying there. Some of the courses were wonderful; being exposed to Washington was wonderful. The connections and friendships that I made at Georgetown changed my entire life. But there were problems at Georgetown that later disappeared.

Q: Well, it was all male at that time.

McCORMACK: There were a few women in my classes, but it was mostly male. The place changed, though, from top to bottom within ten years.

Q: Was Father Walsh doing his thing as school counselor?

McCORMACK: He may have been, but I had no contact with him. I was in the College of Arts and Sciences.

Q: Although you had been told about the Foreign Service, this wasn't your career focus at the time?

McCORMACK: I went to Washington with an idea that I might do this, but I also thought I might go into medicine. I wasn't sure what I wanted to do. I did know that I wanted to study in Washington. Of course I am very happy that I did. But as I say, many of my classmates were not happy about the Georgetown of 1963. As we were receiving our diplomas, I noticed a small fire burning a few steps from the stage in the campus yard. As the students were given their diplomas and alumnus cards, many walked on and threw their cards into the open fire.

Some of the students thought they had been cheated. For example, we had one required philosophy course in which a priest's lectures consisted of reading the textbook. It turned people off.

Q: This was a little early before the feeling of revolt, wasn't it?

McCORMACK: There was a feeling of disillusionment. Some in the administration at the university were openly distressed about the alienation that was obvious in the class of 1963. This was a time when everything in America was in transition. Some things moved for the better, such as race relations, and some things moved for the worse. The culture coarsened. Georgetown was one of those institutions that moved vastly for the better. Today it is one of the top universities in the country.

Q: What about the Kennedy phenomenon during this time? How did that hit? You came from a Republican background, but here was a young charismatic Catholic as president.

McCORMACK: His idea that everyone should engage in public service struck a responsive chord in my generation. In those days, most young people thought highly of Kennedy, except the really hard-shell Republicans, and there were few in my age group in Georgetown. The people I was around thought he was a pretty good guy.

Q: Did you get involved in campus politics at all?

McCORMACK: Not at all.

Q: Debating?

McCORMACK: No. Let me tell you what happened to me at Georgetown and where I spent my time. Sitting next to me when I was a freshman was a young man who was having trouble with English. I thought he was German, but he turned out to be a Belgian. I invited him to spend Thanksgiving vacation with my family in Bradford and to see a different part of America. So we drove 300 miles northeast and spent a very agreeable week in Bradford.

When I returned, I received a phone call a few days later from my new Belgian friend, Boudouin Scheyven, inviting me to lunch. He gave me his address and telephone number. It turned out his father was the Belgian Ambassador, Baron Louis Scheyven. We had a somewhat intimidating, agreeable formal lunch at 2300 Foxhall Road. Gradually these people became a second family to me.

Later, they gave me a key to the embassy. I spent a lot of time in that residence and also visited them in Belgium in the summers. The ambassador and his family taught me diplomacy: everything from painting, ballet, opera, history, languages, to how the various intelligence services work. My friend Boudouin was not interested in a diplomatic career, but I was.

Baron Scheyven was happy to have an interested ear. He had two PhDs and had served as the Chargé in Beijing in 1941, number two in the embassy in Paris, commissioner in Germany, and the senior career official in the Belgian Foreign Service as under secretary. He spoke Arabic, Mandarin, German, French, and English, had written a book on China, and had an incredible collection of Chinese antiques.

His beautiful wife, Evelyn, was from a prominent Swiss family and had been one of the great concert pianists of Europe before she married "Uncle Louis." She had tremendous humanitarian instincts and later wrote children's stories. My relationship with this family has lasted for over 40 years. Their grandchildren have come to spend time with us in McLean, and I will be going shortly to the wedding of my godson, Benjamin, in Brussels.

You can imagine the original culture shock of coming as I did from Bradford, Pennsylvania, a small town where I spent much of my free time in the woods with my Irish setter, fly rod, or a shotgun. It took a while to learn the protocol, but gradually over time it became more natural.

Later their son, Boudouin, my best friend, died of cancer shortly after receiving his PhD from Columbia University with high honors in economics. But his two surviving sisters are still close, particularly the younger one, Marie Catherine. This family was in Washington for ten years from 1959 to 1969 as I went from an eighteen-year-old college freshman to a White House staff member. I owe the Scheyven family an enormous debt. They greatly enriched my life.

Q: Particularly early on, were you getting their point in view of looking at Americans? For most of us this is a little hard—to see how we appear in other people's eyes.

McCORMACK: They were very pro-American and absolutely candid. They hosted dinners with such people as Dean Rusk, Robert McNamara, and Allen Dulles. I sat as often as I could at the foot of the table and listened to their conversations.

Q: Did this whet your appetite for diplomacy?

McCORMACK: Yes, it also made me realize that I could play in that game although I needed to learn a lot more. Years later Herman Kahn, a great think tank figure of the time, said the following to me: "Do not become a specialist. Learn about war, learn about politics, learn about different regions, learn languages, learn history, learn economics, and build the broadest intellectual base that you possibly can. If you do this, your career will advance more slowly than it would if you were to become a narrow expert. But it will allow you to make integrated judgments later in your life. You will peak at a higher level, and you will be more useful as a public servant."

Q: Very good advice.

McCORMACK: I might add concerning my Belgian friends, never once did a Belgian diplomat come to me later when I rose in various official positions and say, "I am a friend of Uncle Louis." Some subsequent Belgian ambassadors never even knew of my relationship to their distinguished predecessor and his family.

Q: As you were going through this, were you getting a feel for how the political system in Washington works?

McCORMACK: Yes. You could hear the reality of things at the dinner table. At that time the Congo was an explosive issue in Washington. Many key U.S. officials were involved with Belgium. Uncle Louis and his wife were very attractive people, and many influential individuals came to dinner and discussed these issues. Some of these discussions—such as those during the Cuban Missile Crisis were dramatic indeed.

From the bottom of the table, I heard about many things that were going on in Washington. I knew, for example, far earlier than most, the actual nature of some of the things that were going on over at the White House. The problems between President Kennedy and his wife were occasionally the stuff of gossip at the dinner table. But one didn't speak about it in public, which is how things were handled in those days.

Q: We are talking about a different world.

McCORMACK: A completely different world.

Q: During this time, while you were still at Georgetown, was there concern about civil rights?

McCORMACK: Yes, as a matter of fact. In those days if a young black were seen in the Georgetown neighborhood in the evening, the police might well pick him up and take him out of the area. Of blacks, only maids could shop at Garfinkels department store when I came to Washington in 1959. This was a southern town. That changed dramatically.

I remember Dean Rusk telling people later about the Carter human rights policy: "You know, all this talk on human rights is embarrassing—the hypocrisy of it all. I can remember when black ambassadors used to ask me where they could get a haircut in Washington, D.C. That wasn't so long ago. Now we presume to set the standards of virtue for the rest of the world."

That was Washington at the time, and like everything else, it was in transition.

Q: What was your major at Georgetown?

McCORMACK: English and philosophy.

Q: By the time you got out of there, you say you were pretty unhappy about Georgetown. Had you thought about going somewhere else?

McCORMACK: I actually did go for one semester to Gannon College in Erie, PA, partly because my father had recurring cancer and I wanted to be closer to home. My father fortunately recovered and I was back in Georgetown the following semester. Georgetown was a far more interesting school than the little college I attended in Erie for one semester. I was not among those who burned their alumni cards.

Q: Where were your classmates from high school going? Were they going off to different places?

McCORMACK: They went to different places. My closest friend, Tom Slivinski, went to Lehigh, got a PhD in computer science, and became a millionaire. The valedictorian of my class, Tom Bissett, also went to Georgetown, roomed with me, and later became a physician. Other classmates also did well.

Q: So you weren't isolated to that extent. I mean people were using this as a place to get out into the world.

McCORMACK: You could go anywhere with an education from Bradford High School in 1959. At Georgetown I didn't have to take any freshmen English classes. I dispensed with them just by taking the exams.

Q: In 1963 you graduated. What then?

McCORMACK: I took the written Foreign Service exam and passed it. By then I could speak basic German and Spanish but felt that I needed graduate courses and more advanced language courses. After graduating from Georgetown I went to the University of Fribourg in Switzerland, which is bilingual: French and German. I was planning to go there for a year or so, but some of the professors urged me to enter the PhD program. So I stayed on for nearly three years.

Q: So you were at Fribourg from '63 to '66.

McCORMACK: That's right.

Q: How did you find the city of Fribourg and the university at that time?

McCORMACK: It was a rather conservative Catholic university. It was a quiet place in a very picturesque part of Switzerland. I had tremendous difficulties my first six months because I had trouble following my bilingual classes. After class I would go to the library and look up every single unknown word from the day's lectures. Then I spent the rest of the evening reading the subject of every lecture in the *Encyclopedia Britannica* or *Colliers* or *Americana*. I usually avoided American students and socialized mainly with Europeans so I could learn the languages and culture.

In 1964 the chancellor of the university retired. He lived in a villa near the university in Fribourg. I was offered his quarters, so I stayed for the next two years with the von Hornstein family in elegant splendor, waited on hand and foot by an old servant. But I never worked so hard before. I mastered those languages. I also traveled to Africa, where I began research for my dissertation. I spent five months in Kenya, Ethiopia, and Uganda.

Q: You might explain what your dissertation was on.

McCORMACK: Yes. I noticed that when the British left their former colonies there was often an explosion, whether it was the Catholics and the Protestants in Ireland or the Hindus and Moslems in India. I realized that they had given minority groups preferences. With British power plus a key minority group behind them, they would rule the majority. I thought I would study how this system worked and chose to study a minority group that had grown up entirely under colonial rule, so there would be no question of historic ethnic tensions. I knew the Indians (Asians) had come to East Africa to build the railroad in the late 19th century

The Asians in Kenya were extremely cooperative with me. I had access to all the historical documents that the Indian Congress had saved in Kenya. I also spent months hitchhiking around East Africa.

Q: What was your impression of Kenya at that time?

McCORMACK: Bear in mind that 1964 was a year of transition in Kenya from British rule. There was still a major presence of the old upper class British families that had come to the playground of East Africa. The government had changed, but not much else. There was still some violence in the north of Kenya. In fact I was nearly killed near Moyali by Somalis. They were attacking truck convoys and so on. The next convoy that came after us was ambushed and they killed everybody in the passenger truck.

Elsewhere the externals remained: Victoria Park in Nairobi was beautiful. Nairobi and broader Kenya were exactly as the British had shaped it, and it was at its peak. Jomo Kenyatta, who of course had grown up in the freedom struggle, was a highly intelligent man and he kept things moving in a stable transition for a considerable period. So I have happy memories of that time.

Q: I have never been there, but was it Happy Valley, where a lot of the expatriate British, and remittance men and women were sent to keep them out of their families' hair in Great Britain.

McCORMACK: Well it was, in part, the playground of the idle rich, but there were others who worked hard to build a new life. I was there basically to learn and listen. I also got to know some of the early settlers, the early white settlers, who had moved into the highlands. I was sometimes a guest in their homes. They would tell me the histories of the early years. It was fascinating. When you get immersed in Africa at that age as I did, it gets into your blood and it never leaves.

Q: Were you picking up any reverberations of what was happening in Kenya, and what was happening in Tanganyika and then Tanzania, with Julius Nyerere, who took quite a different sort of a London School of Economics extreme socialist tack, whereas in Kenya they were pursuing the old and tried system? Were you seeing a conflict there?

McCORMACK: Yes, I was. The conflict was the different visions of how to organize an economy. Even in those days I felt that, while Nyerere was a decent man, his socialist rule was not going to come to a good end. I remember many years later discussing Nyerere's role at a conference at the Ditchley House in England. The same amount of foreign investment came into Malawi and Tanzania. In Malawi, people were fed and the place prospered. It was also a typical strong-man regime, but most of the money that came in was private investment. In the case of Tanzania, the money that came in was Swedish conscience money. It went to fund idealistic but impractical socialist projects that eventually almost wrecked the economy of the country. They are still recovering from that period. That was a time of experimentation. Different people were trying different models of development to see what worked and what did not work.

The "third option" in those days was Nyerere's socialism. But the truth of the matter is that it didn't work very well, partly because governments don't run businesses very effectively. They don't run farms very effectively. As Secretary of State George Shultz later said to me, "Properties run by governments lack the eye of the owner. The owner notices when the house needs to be painted."

Q: What was your impression of the native Kenyan who was coming up in government?

McCORMACK: I stayed at the YMCA in Nairobi. That was a big multiracial facility where you had many good people. In those days it was very spiffy. There were in residence many young blacks who were going into the government, as well as young Asians. There were also a few white people like me. It was a good multiracial mix of people with whom you could have engaging discussions. They were part of a tiny elite on top of a very large uneducated group of people belonging to mutually antagonistic tribes.

Q: Well, back to Switzerland. Did you get any feel in this period of time for how the Swiss viewed America?

McCORMACK: Yes. At that time, many were not happy about the Vietnam War. Most of Europe was not happy about the Vietnam War. There was sympathy, however, for our struggle with the Soviet Union. The Swiss did in fact cooperate with us on some sensitive matters. There was a sense that if things got tough and war came, they would be with us. The Swiss are the most capitalistic of all countries. They were basically our friends, but it was a tightly run little society.

Q: Was there any concern at that time that you were able to pick up about Switzerland's role during WWII?

McCORMACK: What I heard about those days was how they all lost weight. They all had to grow vegetables in their backyard. There was a constant preoccupation with food. Bear in mind that 1963 was less than 20 years after the war. They still had bunkers facing the German frontier. When you came in from Basil with your car, you had to pass two or three different levels of bunkers that were still there on the odd chance that maybe the Russians might come down through Germany.

The Swiss took their military training very seriously. You could see them practicing in the mountains in the summer. I liked to trout fish and hike in the mountains and would sometimes see young soldiers with their units, practicing with their rifles and riding on their bicycles. They all had their rifles in their houses. They all took military service very seriously in those days because they believed that, if they had not been a well-armed group of people, Hitler would have come in and taken them over. That may well have been true. Hitler was gobbling up everything else. I believe the Swiss cooperated with the Germans only to the degree they felt they had to in order to avoid an invasion.

I remember going to an upper class engagement party in Germany where one of my Swiss friends became engaged to the daughter of an industrialist in the Rhineland. The Swiss brought his friends, dressed in their Swiss army uniforms. All the Germans by contrast wore black tie. The father of the bride to be was not a happy man that day.

The fact of the matter was that the Swiss resented the Germans. The very idea that you hear from some these days that most Swiss somehow liked Hitler is utter nonsense. The vast majority hated him. They feared him because he commanded a monstrous military machine. Stu Eizenstat, the former Under Secretary of State, is a friend of mine. He has been active on all these WWII issues involving Switzerland. We have had quite candid discussions on that subject.

To understand Swiss behavior during WWII you have to understand the horror of the times. For almost everybody in Europe in 1939, Hitler was a nightmare, an absolute nightmare. This included many traditional German families. The concentration camps in 1939 were already full of German Jews and the German political opponents of Hitler's regime.

Q: How did you find the university system at Fribourg? How were the classes and the tests done?

McCORMACK: The classes were open and some were seminars. You didn't have to go to class. In the case of the Swiss PhD, the big test is your final exam at the end of three years, where they test you on your three-year work in the course of a three-hour oral interview. You either pass or fail. They test you on everything that you have read or studied in three years. What they want to know is not what you learned and remembered for 24 hours, but what you have integrated as a permanent part of your knowledge. So, knowing that, I worked as hard as I have ever worked in my life during those three years.

After passing my PhD oral exam with honors, I was later offered a teaching assistantship by a senior professor at Tübingen University in Germany. I declined it because by then I had decided on a career in public service, but I appreciated the offer.

Q: In this time, was there a "significant other" at any point? Were you married?

McCORMACK: No, I was not married, but I was privileged to have a remarkable German girl friend, Sophia Reinhart van Guelpen, whom I had first met in Washington and who also studied in Fribourg.

"THE POLITICAL SIDE"

Q: Then in '66 you came back.

McCORMACK: Yes, that is right.

Q: What did you do?

McCORMACK: I was debating whether to pursue the Foreign Service opportunity after passing the written test. I went to my old friend Ambassador Scheyven, who said, "I think rather than going into the Foreign Service, you would find it more challenging to go into the political side of foreign policy. If you do this, you will find there will be times where people will not return your phone calls when your party is out of power." But he said, "There may be times when you can actually help guide the direction of your great country. I think you will find it interesting."

I thought about it a little bit and I talked to a couple of my other friends. Congressman Mel Laird's people in the House of Representatives at the time were trying to rebuild the party after the Goldwater election debacle of 1964, and they were looking for a few people like me.

Q: Mel Laird had been Secretary . . .

McCORMACK: No, before that. He was a congressman from Wisconsin, and the intellectual leader of the Republicans in the House of Representatives. He was what you would call a moderate conservative, extremely intelligent, extremely active and forceful. He helped Congressman Ford become the minority leader. Bill Prendergast was his chosen instrument at the House Republican Conference.

They hired me to help run the summer intern program, and then offered me an administrative assistantship to one of the congressmen. That summer I carried out several projects, including a major research project on the Vietnam War policy, which involved interaction with the Vietnamese ambassador and others.

The local Project Head Start was under-enrolled that year. So I organized all the Republican interns to go out and recruit black youngsters to fill up the empty classrooms. Our effort received big headlines in all the local newspapers. It was quite an interesting summer. At the end, the Republicans encouraged me to pursue a political path in the foreign policy area. But I was also offered a position on the Peace Corps staff. Warren Wiggins, the deputy director of the Peace Corps, and former Navy Commander Joe Farrell were trying to get someone to help run a big global school building program to carry out a pledge by President Johnson to build 1000 Peace Corps schools in the Third World.

Q: This was President Johnson.

McCORMACK: Yes, 1966. In his State of the Union message, he promised that the Peace Corps would build these thousand schools with the voluntary contributions of American school children. Unlike today's world, every presidential promise in those days was enforced. The Peace Corps wanted somebody to help organize the fundraising. I spent the next year or so successfully raising money for this project.

Q: How did you go about that?

McCORMACK: Mass mailings organized by Young and Rubicam, a prominent ad agency, and visits to high schools. I organized young Peace Corps people to speak to high schools around the nation. Then we convinced some of the governors to sponsor whole areas. For example, Governor Romney of Michigan adopted Tanzania and we built 100 schools in Tanzania. By the time I finished with this project, we couldn't generate the overseas projects fast enough to spend the money. Then I did some troubleshooting for other Peace Corps projects that were having problems.

Later, a friend in Congress called me to help a man who was running for mayor in Philadelphia, Arlen Specter. They needed somebody to write his white paper on race relations. So I ended my Peace Corps activity and went to Philadelphia. I spent the next five or six months writing Specter's white paper on race relations, with a heavy emphasis on education and equal opportunity.

Q: How did you go about looking at race relations in Philadelphia?.

McCORMACK: I talked to many people, both the impacted people and other experts in the area. I concluded that obviously education was an important dimension. So I proposed a program for improving the education of the black youngsters. Specter liked the white paper and issued it. He lost the election by less than10,000 votes.

Then friends suggested that maybe I should go to Vietnam and consider some of the problems there. So I became the head of operations research for Philco-Ford in their Southeast Asia headquarters in Saigon, Vietnam.

Q: For whom?

McCORMACK: Philco-Ford Corporation. I originally worked mainly on the war refugee problems in Vietnam, but I had broader responsibilities. I was based in Saigon where I worked at headquarters but traveled widely in Laos, Cambodia, Thailand, Indonesia, and Malaysia.

The Tet Offensive occurred while I was there. I was also working as an analyst and sending papers with suggestions to embassy people. At one point, Ambassador Robert Komer, who was in charge of the pacification program, asked me to become the deputy science advisor to the commander of U.S. forces in Vietnam, with responsibilities for coordinating all the soft science research being done in Vietnam by such groups as the Rand Corporation. This was a GS-18, PL 313, position. I agreed to do it.

This was, of course, a time of tremendous turmoil. I said I would take the job under the condition that I could return to the U.S. and recruit five or six top people of my own generation to work with me. That was agreed. So I flew back to the United States in July. Then a congressional hiring freeze passed.

I recruited six of the ablest people of our generation. We sat in the Pentagon and sat and sat. Komer, who was kind of an irascible fellow, began sending outraged cables demanding that I be sent back, but the Pentagon bureaucracy just wouldn't move. I later discovered that some functionary in personnel had said, "How can a 27-year old man take GS-18 responsibility levels?" So they used the excuse of the hiring freeze to delay. So after a month of this, I gave up and helped coordinate the Vietnam issue for Nixon in his '68 campaign headquarters in New York. My six friends all went off to brilliant careers in other areas.

Q: Well, let's talk about the time you were in Saigon. What were you doing when the Tet Offensive hit?

McCORMACK: I was living in Saigon in a very exposed section of the city when the attack occurred. There was a lot of gunfire in the neighborhood where I lived.

Q: Where was that?

McCORMACK: I lived right between Saigon and Cholon. You remember Cholon?

Q: That was the Chinese part?

McCORMACK: I was right on the border of Cholon. I was staying in an apartment building owned by a Vietnamese, Mr. Thu, a very nice man. During the entire Tet offensive we had Viet Cong all around us.

Q: Where there was a bunch of heavy fighting?

McCORMACK: Heavy fighting. In any case, on the day of the Tet attack, I was curious to see what was happening because you could see smoke coming up in different places and could hear gunfire. I walked down to the Bachelor Officers Quarters, where I often ate. Someone explained to me what was happening, so I began moving around town, going from one area to the other. I went to see if the U.S. embassy was still under fire. I could see big piles of smoldering wreckage in front of the embassy.

The Viet Cong still had people who were hidden in the area there, and they were firing. Then I went to the presidential palace, where there was another problem. As I was walking around the corner to the presidential palace, which was on my right, I stepped over a bunch of bodies that were on the sidewalk and there was absolute silence. I looked around, and all of a sudden gunfire erupted. I dove into a little alley, where the Korean embassy was located. It turned out the Viet Cong were occupying a large building next to this embassy, which was immediately to the left of the presidential palace. There were two brick walls along the driveway, where the ambassador's car was normally parked. That is where Korean marines were crouched, attempting to deal with the Viet Cong in the high-rise, 30 yards to the left.

They were firing at each other, and I was there with them. Of course, except for a pistol, I was unarmed, but it went on for quite a while and it was very loud. Walls were shaking and people were screaming. As it turned out, a CBS camera crew was filming us from across the yard of the presidential palace with a telescopic lens. During one period when the gunfire was particularly intense, I leaned up against the wall and just put my fingers in my ears because the noise was absolutely deafening. Tank fire eventually dealt with our problem. All this appeared on the CBS evening news, generating letters from personal friends who saw the footage. The same footage was run again years later as "Letters from Vietnam," a special CBS program on the war.

Fortunately the Viet Cong never got into my apartment building. After a week, they were pushed back. Then I began traveling around Vietnam, Laos, and Cambodia. Herman Kahn was doing assessments for DARPA, and I was put on his plane. He and I traveled all over the region, interviewing military people to learn what might be done.

Q: What was your impression at this point, where public opinion was beginning to move against the policy in the United States? In the field, what was your impression about the value of our commitment there and how things were going?

McCORMACK: I thought it was a winnable proposition under certain circumstances, but I was not always impressed by what I saw at the upper levels of our operation over there. It was also very obvious to me that we were more enthusiastic about winning that war than a lot of the Vietnamese were by then. It was largely an American war. There was a tremendous amount of dedication by the U.S. officer corps: captains, colonels, majors, lieutenants. There were many good people there. At the time, though, I felt our strategy of graduated escalation was flawed and not well thought out. But in those days, I took the domino theory seriously. We all did. As I traveled around other countries in the region, it was very clear to me that even Thailand was potentially vulnerable. Malaysia had just come through a very close call with Communist insurgents.

Q: During the trouble, what did they call this? I can't remember what they called it.

McCORMACK: I did not by any means think that it was a hopeless proposition, but I felt that we might not win it operating the way we were. Herman Kahn came up with his idea of building a barrier around Vietnam with moats and fences. Herman was a very smart man and I was very fond of him. I kept in touch with him for years after that.

Some of his ideas were brilliant. Some of them, however, were not. After returning from our fact-finding trip around Vietnam, Herman addressed the officers of the U.S. command in Vietnam. He started out by saying, "The reason the war is going badly is because of the shortcomings of the men in this room." Some of the officers actually got up and walked out. But in any case, I learned a lot selectively from Kahn. He was quite an interesting man with a tremendously eclectic mind and a very engaging personality.

Q: When you came back, what sort of things were you working on?

McCORMACK: When I returned, I eventually was recruited as part of the Nixon campaign staff in 1968 at the New York headquarters. I worked mainly on the foreign affairs side, including drafting papers on Biafra, Vietnam, and the 1948 Dewey campaign. Nixon liked those papers very much.

Q: How did you find the spirit of the people around Nixon at that time?

McCORMACK: There were two groups. There was the group of advance men, the Haldeman-Ehrlichman operation, who referred to the other group disparagingly as the "think tank types." There was a power struggle between the "think tank types" and the advance men, and the advance men won. But I met some tremendous people: Lee Huebner, who later became publisher of the *International Herald Tribune*; John Price, who became a top banker; Ray Price, who is now president of the New York Economic Club. Pat Buchanan, Bill Safire, and Alan Greenspan were also there.

It was a very eclectic and interesting group of people. I learned a great deal from them. Dick Whalen, who had been one of the editors of *Fortune* magazine, resigned after the big dust-up between the think tank types and the advance men and wrote an unflattering book called *Catch the Falling Flag*. He didn't feel the advance men had sufficient vision.

Whalen didn't like the advance men. He thought they had risen beyond their abilities to provide wise policy advice, however useful they might be in running a campaign.

Q: How about when you were looking at Biafra. It tried to split away. It is hard today to reconstruct the feeling, particularly of what you might call the glitterati. A lot of people were very supportive of the Biafran movement.

McCORMACK: I encouraged Nixon to support them. Nigeria was a polyglot of different groups and tribes, as you know. The Biafrans were another of the groups that had prospered during the colonial period. When the British left, their status was reduced. They struggled and were crushed.

The Organization of African Unity was founded on the premise that once you started redrawing borders of African countries on a tribal basis, there would be no end to it. If I were writing the press release on Biafra today, I would write it differently.

Q: Well it is interesting how this movement really did catch on. For one thing, I think the Biafrans were supreme public relations people.

McCORMACK: They were.

Q: They played the United States and the Brits like a violin.

McCORMACK: Yes. The war was a brutal one. But you will notice a great positive lesson. The victorious Nigerian leaders ended the Biafran War in the same spirit that Lincoln wanted to end the U.S. Civil War, to reconcile the country. There was no revenge. Thus the country was reconciled to itself. Who could have predicted that?

Q: *How did you find the campaign, particularly in the earlier part where the intellectual foundations were being laid? How did you find Nixon at that time? Was he around much?*

McCORMACK: Yes, he was around, but he was a distant presence to me. He was reported to be very interested in the papers I was writing and sent encouraging messages that he would not forget them. I was a very junior person on that staff.

I should note in passing that I had some contacts with Richard Nixon beginning from that time until he died. I was at his last public presentation three weeks before he passed on. He talked about Russia. He had just made an extensive trip there. Nixon was a constant work in progress and became a wiser and better person over time, like other former presidents. This was a man who had well known insecurities and was never really comfortable with the upper class of the eastern wing of the Republican Party. They were also rivals for power: Main Street versus Wall Street. Politics is a tough business, very close to war in its conception and execution.

Nixon was not your hail-fellow-well-met. But he was a much abler and nicer man than his critics gave him credit for. He nearly died after he left the White House. His physician reportedly slapped him in the face in the hospital at one point and said, "Come back, Richard, come back." He was that close to death. But he lived and decided to contribute the best he could to the country as an ex-president.

He had vast experience in foreign affairs. He was widely read and traveled, and he was an excellent analyst. He was widely respected abroad. Gradually over time he redeemed himself, first in his own eyes, which was so important, then gradually in the eyes of many others. When he died, Bob Dole actually wept at Nixon's funeral while he was trying to deliver a funeral oration. I can tell you no one would have cried if Nixon had died the year he left the White House, except his family. He had a close relationship with his family, unlike many politicians. As an ex-president, Nixon truly became a valuable statesman and advisor.

Q: It is interesting that in my interviews, Nixon rates much higher with the professionals of the Foreign Service. I think at the time he felt estranged from the Foreign Service. Looking back now, though, the professionals of the Foreign Service say, "Hell, this guy knew his stuff."

McCORMACK: Part of the strain between Nixon and the Foreign Service happened when he was vice president and later after he had lost the election of 1960. He would travel around the world. He was not always well received in every embassy, but he remembered those Foreign Service officers who did assist him courteously.

Q: I know Henry Tasca headed our embassy in Morocco and received Nixon very well.

McCORMACK: Yes. The second problem he had with the Foreign Service came during the White House years. Henry Kissinger, of course, was the national security advisor under him. Henry came in with a very high IQ and with a tremendous amount of ambition but with certain insecurities of his own. He was trying to pull power into the White House, which is what Nixon wanted. Bill Rogers and the State Department resisted. There was a constant fight between Rogers and Kissinger, with Rogers representing the institutional interests of the State Department. Obviously Kissinger pushed for his own interests and views, and the president's when they coincided, as was usually but not always the case.

From time to time the NSA "big ear" would pick up comments from this Foreign Service officer or that Foreign Service officer about policy and the White House. Kissinger was not above getting those things, giving them to the president and using them as a weapon against individual Foreign Service officers, increasing Nixon's own sense of paranoia toward them. He fed it and fed it. I was present for one occasion when this happened at San Clemente.

Q: I must say that Kissinger and Nixon really brought out the worst in each other.

McCORMACK: They brought out the worst and the best, actually. For example, Henry Kissinger sometimes takes credit for Nixon's China initiative, but the fact is the China initiative was proposed in March of 1968 in a *Foreign Affairs* article written by Nixon even before he knew Henry Kissinger. Secondly, Kissinger initially opposed the China initiative, claiming that if we wanted to have any kind of detente with the Russians, they would never forgive us for cozying up to the Chinese. Nixon replied that if we wanted to have any respectful relationship with the Russians, the only way would be to develop some leverage on them through the Chinese.

He forced Kissinger forward on this issue. Of course, so much water has gone over the dam since then that hardly anybody now remembers those early discussions and press debates that were leaked in Evans and Novak articles. In the end, Nixon seemed to resent Kissinger. He felt that Henry was seeking credit for everything good that he had initiated.

Q: Can you talk about the arrival of Henry Kissinger and how he was viewed at the time when you were part of the think tank crowd?

McCORMACK: Well, he was viewed with tremendous resentment by Dick Allen. Dick Allen wanted to be the national security advisor himself. He felt that this had been snatched away from him by Henry, and of course he was outraged about it.

As a matter of fact, when Kissinger went to the White House, Dick, as a consolation prize, was made one of his deputies. But shortly after he arrived at the White House, Kissinger called in Bromley Smith, who was the executive secretary of the National Security Council. He said, "Bromley, I want you to do to Dick Allen what you and Bundy did to me in 1961." Bromley said, "What do you mean?" He said, "You know what I mean." So Dick Allen found himself up on the fourth floor of the EOB (Executive Office Building) and was given modest responsibilities. Three weeks later Bromley Smith was given an adjacent office on the fourth floor of the EOB. Shortly after that, Smith joined me on a transition exercise at the State Department, where I served as Governor Scranton's assistant. Governor Scranton comes from northern Pennsylvania, as I do. He was asked by Nixon to be secretary of state but declined. He never really trusted or liked Nixon, stemming from earlier political clashes and differences between them.

Q: Well he probably was right in a way, because Nixon did not want a powerful secretary of state.

McCORMACK: Scranton did offer to do some part-time tasks for Nixon. One task was to chair the INTELSAT negotiation. I was a special assistant to Scranton during this transition, and for the first few months of the administration I helped organize this project. I got to know Governor Scranton well during that period. We became good friends, a friendship which lasts to this day. Then I was invited to the White House after a few months at State to join the President's Advisory Council on Executive Organization (known as the Ash Council).

Q: We have covered how you got on to the Nixon team in the early times. I don't know if there is anything else we should discuss about the election campaign?

McCORMACK: You could see the election polls between Nixon and Humphrey narrowing and narrowing. The memo I wrote for Nixon in September of that year was called "Dewey's Plunge to Oblivion." It talked about all the mistakes that had been made by the Dewey campaign. After Nixon read this memo, he called all the senior staff to Key Biscayne to organize what he called Operation Extra Effort. Even though at that time they were still ahead in the polls, they eventually won by less than one percent of the vote. Nixon claimed that meeting at Key Biscayne, triggered by my memo, helped make him President.

Q: What was the Dewey thing, overconfidence?

McCORMACK: Overconfidence and the willingness of the other side to be completely ruthless in a political way. Truman called Dewey a Fascist and said he would bring the depression back to the farms. He called the Republicans gluttons of privilege, and on and on. In my memo, I wrote that Democratic Party operatives were unlikely to be any more restrained on tactics in this election than in the past. I concluded there would be a peace offensive shortly before the election. There would be efforts to make it appear that all kinds of problems are going to be solved. Scandals would come to a crescendo three weeks before the election. I urged us to be prepared for the worst.

For me, there was a kind of cocoon-like environment in the campaign. I was free to write my memos, which were read by all the key people. But the older, more experienced people were the ones invited to attend the key meetings. After Nixon began taking note of my memoranda and acting on my recommendations, one insecure and unscrupulous colleague whispered that I was a secret CIA plant and therefore not to be trusted. I later learned that I was not the only victim of this man's character assassination.

The election was won, and I returned to Washington. But I didn't go immediately into the transition staff. I began attending classes in the black schools in Washington, D.C. to see if I could test some of the theories from Specter's campaign. Tommy Corcoran's daughter, Cecily, worked with me for two months to look for ways of testing what could be done to improve education in these schools. One of the things that struck me was how difficult it was to keep quality teachers in that stressful teaching environment.

I thought of a program to provide a big bonus, based on test scores, for a teacher who brings a student's scores up by more than one-year's reading ability in the time that she has the student. My thought was that not only would they have an incentive to work harder, but it would compensate some of the really good people for the difficult working environment. I remember one elementary school principal showing me brass knuckles, knives, and clubs that he had confiscated from the young children.

There were two fifth grade classes in one school that we monitored. One was taught by an amazing black woman who was about 30 years old. She was teaching the children Christmas carols in Swahili. She was even showing the boys how to do karate during the recess period. She had order in her class. I said to myself when I saw her, "You are what I want to clone over and over again."

The other fifth grade class in that school was taught by a white woman who was one year from retirement. She had no control over the class. She resented our being there. When I looked at the achievement test results for those two teachers, they were identical. The average was 14 percentile. When I saw that, I despaired. I absolutely despaired.

Then I identified three or four children in the classes who had done unusually well. I visited the families to see the home environment. You saw in an instant what the difference was. The high achievers were from orderly home environments. Father and mother were present. There were not a lot of beer bottles all over the floor. In some cases, they had previously been to Catholic schools. I realized the problem didn't begin with the schools. It began in the home. It was a kind of chicken and egg problem. I also realized this problem was beyond my ability to solve.

I am, however, still involved with this problem as a member of a volunteer task force forty years later in Washington. The charter school movement has produced some unusual successes. There is much to be learned from the best of them. The greatest challenge in America today, in my judgment, is to do something about the disintegration of families and about the conditions producing large numbers of dysfunctional young people now ending up in jail. It is a national disgrace.

Q: Tell me more about your experience with the Nixon administration. What were some of the issues that were coming up with INTELSAT at that time? This was just at the beginning, but it was a very important beginning.

McCORMACK: It had to do with governance, how the power within INTELSAT would be shared in the private-public partnership. The private side was anxious to maximize its own role and financial situation. When I say the public side, I mean the international public side, because this was for the global satellite communications operation. Naturally, one had to have the cooperation of other governments and other ministries of telecommunications. So this was a long negotiation between governments and the private entity Comsat, which had been organized to provide the technical managing skills and administration of the enterprise.

The sharing of power and revenues and rate making decisions and all this sort of thing were on the table. It was very clear to me that this negotiation was going to take a very long time. I really didn't want to spend the rest of my time in the Nixon administration squabbling between the Comsat people and the minister of telecommunications of Chile. When I was offered a position at the White House with the Ash Council to help reorganize parts of the American government, I accepted. This decision had the full support of Governor Scranton.

I spent the next couple of years on task forces doing such things as reorganizing and strengthening parts of the Executive Office of the President. We were the ones who put the management function in Office of Management and Budget (OMB) and set up the Environmental Protection Agency. We were also heavily involved in setting up NOAA.

Q: You might explain what NOAA was.

McCORMACK: It was the National Oceanic and Atmospheric Administration. It was a great privilege for me to be part of this exercise because I was working with the very able Roy Ash, our chairman, who was then also the president of Litton Industries, and Walter Thayer, who was the publisher of the *International Herald Tribune* and also led the Whitney financial empire in New York. Thayer was also a man of immense integrity, character, and ability. Fred Kappel, the former head of AT&T, Dick Paget from McCormick and Paget consulting firm, George Baker, dean of the Harvard Business School, and John Connally, the former governor of Texas, were also active on the council. It was as able a group of people as I have ever worked with before or since. They assigned me to work on the White House reorganization and to help coordinate the international work of the council.

Q: Obviously, the government can always be made more efficient. But you had another trend going there—within the Nixon White House—of concentrating power. This was very much a Nixon thing, for good or evil, but it was there. And you had people like Haldeman and Ehrlichman. How did the political side intrude on this group of very distinguished people on the council, who were not political but were looking for practical solutions?

McCORMACK: Our group reported directly to the president of the United States and made our recommendations directly to him. The other White House staff sat quietly by while we made our presentations and the president considered his decisions.

Obviously there are two different models for running the U.S. government: the strong cabinet model and the strong White House approach. Nixon was anxious to have a strong White House. This was especially true in the national security area, where he had Kissinger pull in all the policy study groups under the National Security Council. He also took over many of the operations that had previously been delegated to other agencies. It created tremendous ill will and tension between the State Department and the NSC.

In the case of the Bureau of the Budget, Nixon felt there were still too many people from the New Deal there. The Bureau of the Budget was originally set up by Franklin Roosevelt to take power away from the Treasury Department, which Roosevelt felt had mismanaged its responsibilities during the 1920s and thus contributed to the 1929 financial crisis and subsequent depression.

Q: Mellon particularly.

McCORMACK: That's right. Roosevelt wanted to weaken the Treasury Department's power. He created the Securities and Exchange Commission, an independent entity. He pulled the Bureau of the Budget into the Executive Office to assemble the federal budget under presidential aegis. Some of the people who were hired by Roosevelt were still there when Nixon arrived. Nixon was anxious to terminate some of the failed experiments of Johnson's Great Society project. He felt rightly or wrongly that some of the career people in the Bureau of the Budget were too closely wedded to President Johnson's concepts and were using their connections with congressional staff to thwart his desires to make changes.

He wanted to have a layer of political appointees in the Bureau of the Budget who would implement what the president wanted done. That was part of the basis on which the management dimension was added to the Bureau of the Budget. All this caused a lot of tension with the senior career staff of the Bureau of the Budget. Roy Ash subsequently became the head of the Office of Management and Budget, which may have been his original ambition.

There were several matters that I personally was heavily involved with at the Ash Council. I could see there was a lot of tension between the Nixon political appointees and the senior career bureaucrats. I thought much of this was needless and counterproductive. It was also clear to me that some of the career people were more left of center than Republican officials normally are. It was also clear to me that unless there was some way for the political people to work more effectively with the career staff, not much would happen except huge exercises of mutual frustration and press leaks. So I asked the council to allow me to take a month off to study the whole problem of the poor relations between the political appointees and the career people and see if I could develop some recommendations and techniques for improving this situation. They agreed.

I visited some of the best political appointees from former administrations and the present administration, people like former Secretary of Defense Clark Clifford. I talked to some of the smartest senior bureaucrats that I could find in the system. Then I produced a paper called "Advice to Senior Political Appointees on Management of the Bureaucracy," which is kind of a handbook for how a political appointee can come into a position and actually make a useful contribution rather than just mucking up the works or being manipulated by the bureaucracy. The president approved the paper, and it was passed out to new political appointees as part of their White House briefing.

Later in the administration, when a considerably more hostile attitude developed toward the career people, this paper was retracted and a much more intrusive and hostile system was established. By then I was out of the system. However, my paper became part of the curriculum of the Federal Executive Institute at Charlottesville, VA where it remained for more than 20 years.

Q: You are putting your finger on something that I have noticed, that there is always a problem of the career people having to deal with a political appointee, and that some do it well and some don't. But in a way, that is their problem and they have to learn how to make it work. They should have had better training. But the disturbing thing is how many people come in from a political administration like Nixon's with a hostility built in. Normally bureaucrats want to succeed.

McCORMACK: There are two reasons for the problem. One of which is insecurity. If you take a man who has been selling cars in Duluth and you put him into a system where everybody who works for him knows more than he does about the substance of the matter, you are going to have somebody who is potentially nervous about his role. That is one point. The second is that sometimes you get a situation where many people in the career system are opposed to decisions of the president. That is one of the justifications for having a layer of political people in the system.

We do, after all, have a democracy. It is very easy in a large agency to thwart a political decision or to delay it unless there is an ongoing accountability system established. I have subsequently been in the U.S. government for a very long time. If you get some cockamamie order from the top that doesn't make any sense, there are ways to slow it up so that an appeal can be made to reconsider. On the other hand, if you get some well positioned, highly opinionated person who simply disagrees with policy decisions, he can do the same thing. Obviously, career officials who make personal decisions on what they are going to carry out and what they are not going to carry out are themselves of different levels of sophistication, judgment, and ability.

Our system has been set up in such a way that when we have an election of the president, who campaigns on a certain agenda and comes into office, he is given enough management tools so he can influence the system rather than just being absorbed by it. There is good and there is bad in this. The good is that from time to time change is necessary. In fact, our four-year elections are where the American people get an opportunity to hear both sides, and many issues are debated. Then they vote for team A or team B to implement its campaign program. That is how our democracy works. The bad part of it is that not every speech on a campaign trail that gets rousing cheers is sound policy. This is obviously an issue that could lead to a very long discussion where the press, Congress, and other agencies get involved in debating controversial initiatives.

The point I want to make is that I did address this complex issue, and this paper is still being circulated 30 years later. To my astonishment the current head of the White House personnel office, Clay Johnson, was interviewed by *The Washington Post* during the transition. He cited my paper as one of two things he had found most helpful. I haven't a clue where he got it. There have been thousands of copies of that paper distributed throughout our system. In fact when I was a scholar many years later at the Woodrow Wilson International Center for Scholars in 1992, the National Governors Association staff called to ask if I would update it. So I revised it modestly. I found that I had very little to add to the original paper, except on press relations. This revised paper is on file at the Woodrow Wilson Center in Washington, D.C.

Q: You mentioned the environmental issues. Nixon is often seen as a right-wing person, and yet so many basic reforms came then. Could you explain some of the thinking?

McCORMACK: While Nixon was perceived by some as "right wing," he was not a right-wing type. He was generally a moderate, main street Republican, looking for practical solutions to difficult problems. The public perception of him and the man himself are very different in some important ways. Both Herb Stein and Pat Buchanan were important components of his White House. Nixon wanted to hear different perspectives before he made decisions.

Nixon was also a politician and understood that you had to get elected before you could actually be in power. He did what he felt he had to do to get from point A to point B on the political scene, with one important exception, which needs to be noted. That was in the 1960 elections, where he narrowly lost to Jack Kennedy. It was very clear to him that a legal challenge could have been made in Illinois on the Kennedy election. There were shenanigans on a huge scale that occurred in Chicago, with the cemeteries voting in large numbers. Many Republicans were urging Nixon to challenge the election results in court in Illinois, just as the Democrats later did in the 2000 Florida recount. He refused to do this. He said that it would de-legitimize the president and poison his presidency. He acted as he did because he felt that it was in the country's best interest, for which he received very little public credit. It also shows another side to the man that helps explains why Nixon had loyal friends as well as bitter enemies. There was another side to this man, perhaps coming from his Quaker mother, which was an important part of his makeup that not everybody saw or understood.

At that time the environment was an increasingly important issue with the American people. Many rivers were badly polluted. Air in our cities was often ghastly. People wanted changes. The president wanted to be out front on these environmental issues, and we were given the task of coming up with some organizational solutions. Doug Costle was the team chairman for this project, and he and the Ash Council basically developed the plans for setting up the Environmental Protection Agency.

My key tasks on the Ash Council included: 1) developing the plans for the council on International Economic Policy, 2) helping to reorganize the Special Trade Representative's Office, 3) helping to set up the Domestic Council, and 4) strengthening the Executive Office of the President. Toward the end of my two-year involvement, a super cabinet project was proposed to bring the secretaries of State, Defense, and Treasury and the Attorney General into the Executive Office of the President. The idea was to make them presidential people rather than representatives of their agencies and supposedly vulnerable to being captured by their agency staffs. My view was there were just too many vested congressional interests that would oppose this concentration of power and that it was thus a waste of time. I said, "Everything else we have proposed thus far has succeeded. But this initiative will never fly." I could see on their faces that the members of the Ash Council, all of whom I respected and liked very much, were disappointed that I felt that way.

Q: It was sort of like going to the metric system.

McCORMACK: This was an effort to bring all that power into the Executive Office of the President. Of course you could make a case for it. One of the reasons I felt it would not be successful was that it would require major congressional reorganization and support. We didn't control the Congress. This would shatter the existing committee systems of Congress. It would create tremendous resentment and resistance by powerful committee chairmen.

The Ash Council reports were never circulated. They went to the president, and each member of the Ash Council was given his personal copy of the reports. I don't believe there were more than 15 or 20 copies ever made. One of the members of the council, however, was kind enough to give me one of the rare books with the understanding that it would be kept in confidence. So I am one of the few people who actually have a complete set of the Ash Council documents. Reading them again, you feel proud now of the quality of the analyses. But it reflected not just the work of young people like myself, although we strove mightily. Rather it reflected the best thinking of the cream of the 1969 corporate America's elite.

Q: Also in a way, and I hate to say this, I think it was a different breed of cat in those days who took a little longer view of their role in society than is reflected in corporate America today.

McCORMACK: Well it was a different era, a completely different era. In any case, to have had the opportunity to learn from these men was immensely valuable to me.

Q: I would like to return to one thing that pertains to foreign policy. You said there were problems with the Special Trade Representative. Could you explain what you were working on?

McCORMACK: Nixon had naturally replaced President Johnson's people in the White House Trade Office, including Bill Roth from San Francisco, whom I had known socially from the Belgian embassy dinners and liked very much. His successor was Carl Gilbert, an elderly gentleman from the Gillette Razor Company. There was no real mandate for major trade legislation in those days. Many of the senior staff had been dismissed, and things were not going very well in the trade office. Because there was some squabbling going on, Ambassador Gilbert called his friends on the Ash Council and said, "Could you send someone over here to help me reorganize this place?" I was the one they sent. So what I basically did was talk to all the smart people who had been fired. I also went to see Phil Trezise, the assistant secretary of state, and Harold Malmgren, who was another very smart man. With their help and that of others I produced a paper, which was then implemented.

When I was asked to develop plans and rationale for the Council of International Economic Policy, I did the same thing. I simply went to the best people who were or had been in the system, had a high level of technical knowledge, and drew heavily on them. The man who was most helpful to me was again Hal Malmgren, one of the former assistant trade negotiators. Hal worked at a regular day job. Then he would come to the White House at 5:00 in the afternoon and he would work until 10:00 at night, day after day. The result of this collaboration was a lengthy paper plus a summary with organizational and policy recommendations. This was later approved by the President.

After President Nixon had approved setting up the Council on International Economic Policy, I was asked to recommend possible candidates to head up the new office in the White House. I naturally sought the best advice possible, and I called the office of the then Chairman of the Federal Reserve Board of Governors, William McChesney Martin to seek an appointment.

The appointment was arranged for the following day. What I did not realize was that this was Martin's final day in office after having presided as the longest serving Chairman in the history of the Federal Reserve. I was, in fact, his final appointment, and after a fascinating two-hour discussion, he left the office for the last time, headed for a long trip to the Galapagos Islands to decompress.

When I asked him what kind of person we should recruit to head up the new office, he responded: "If you want this new office to be relevant, do not appoint an academic economist, and particularly avoid econometricians." Instead, he recommended that we recruit someone who "had broad personal reach in the American and global economy, who understood how markets operated, and who was able through a network of personal contacts to anticipate developments before they were finally reported in the official statistics.

He went on to say: "We have fifty econometricians working for us at the Fed. They are all located in the basement of this building, and there is a reason why they are there. Their main value to me is to pose questions that I then pass on to my own network of contacts throughout the American economy. The danger with these econometricians is that they don't know their own limitations, and they have a far grater sense of confidence in their analyses than I have found to be warranted. Such people are not dangerous to me because I understand their limitations. They are, however, dangerous to people like you and the politicians because you don't know their limitations, and you are impressed and confused by the elaborate models and mathematics. The flaws in these analyses are almost always imbedded in the assumptions upon which they are based. And that is where broader wisdom is required, a wisdom that these mathematicians generally do not have. You always want such technical experts on tap in positions like this, but never on top."

Let me give you an example of what I mean. When I have a monetary policy decision to make, I get on the telephone and spend four or five days calling informed people around the country to seek their views of supply, demand, wage, and inflation trends. I speak with labor leaders, grain dealers, manufacturers, individuals I respect in the regional Federal Reserve Banks, and others who have their fingers on the pulse of the U.S. economy. Then I go up to New York City and spend two days visiting bankers and corporate leaders and others I trust to seek their advice. The eventual results of these discussions form the basis for my monetary policy decisions. And that is how I operated for many years, with one very sad exception."

A few years ago, as the Vietnam War and Great Society programs were heating up, it was obvious to me that inflationary pressures were building in the American economy, and that a gradual tightening of monetary policy was absolutely necessary to head this off. I sent word over to the White House that this was my intention. Shortly after this, I received a call from President Johnson's office asking me to join him for a discussion at his ranch in Texas. I assumed it was to be meeting of the Quad (Secretaries of the Treasury and Department of Commerce, Chairmen of the Federal Reserve and Council of Economic Advisors).

So I flew down to Texas and drove out to the President's ranch. Much to my surprise when I was shown into the President's living room, there was no one else present. After a few minutes, the President joined me, alone, the two of us, standing.

Without any preliminaries, he said, "Bill, I need your help!" Of course I knew what he had in mind so I started to explain to him what kind of inflationary pressures were building in the American economy, the potential consequences, and why it was necessary to tighten policy to head all of this off.

He responded, "You don't understand. I need your help!" So I made one more effort to explain to him what would happen if we did not promptly start tightening policy. Suddenly he advanced upon me, physically pushing me around the room, and shouting in my face: "Boys are dying in Vietnam, and Bill Martin doesn't care!"

Then, in a regretful tone, Martin concluded: "To my everlasting shame, I finally gave into him . . . . And that's how inflation became imbedded into this economy."

When I returned to the White House, I carefully wrote all this up in a secret sensitive memorandum to Walter Thayer, the member of the Ash Council with whom I worked most closely and an old Wall Street friend of

Chairman Martin. He read the memo very carefully and then said to me: "Dick if this memo leaks, it will be on the front page of every newspaper in the country. We obviously don't want this. So when we have our meeting with the full Council, I am going to circulate your memo around the table and then retrieve it."

The memo never did leak although a few years ago, I did send a summary of it to Ned Gramlich, one of the Governors of the Federal Reserve System, who had previously served as a Fed staff member during the period in question. He later wrote to me: "We knew there was Presidential interference with monetary policy—just didn't know how bad it was."

The White House subsequently recruited Pete Peterson, the former president of Bell and Howell, to run the Council on International Economic Policy. It took a great effort to get him actually appointed to the job because some of the existing White House staff leadership did not want another strong man brought into the White House to compete with them.

Q: Were you feeling the hand of Ehrlichman and Kissinger and all?

McCORMACK: Yes. The president himself had to overrule his staff. We did get Peterson hired. He did make the office work, and they produced very useful reports for a number of years. A key purpose of this whole exercise was to cope with the threatened collapse of the Bretton Woods system. The Bretton Woods system was set up to govern monetary relations among the allied countries after WWII and to help coordinate their balance of payment problems. Because of the demands of the Vietnam War and Great Society, monetary policy was too loose. That, of course, started inflation again and caused excess demand in the United States. Our balance of payments went out of kilter and we started to accumulate debts abroad. The Bretton Woods system simply could not work if a major country like the U.S. did not balance its current account.

The French viewed our monetary policy partly as creating dollars with which to buy up European assets on the cheap, among other things. They began demanding gold. The only way we could actually make the old system work was to bring our current accounts back into balance. So we tried to pull all of our policies together—aid, trade, development, and finance—in one strategic policy unit so that we could leverage all the potential strength of the American economy. The purpose in creating this unit was to ensure that our trade policy was not made in isolation. But in the end, as you well know, the Bretton Woods system did collapse and we closed the gold window.

However, the inflationary pressures and subsequent recession later led to a misguided effort to impose wage and price controls and expand the monetary base. This policy temporarily improved the economy, helped re-elect President Nixon, but quickly imploded after the election, contributing to the Watergate-related pressures that eventually led to the resignation of President Nixon.

When the Republicans left office in 1977, the Council of International Economic Policy was abolished. It subsequently has been re-established under different names and is much smaller. This big White House operation, which was originally conceived to coordinate our global economic strategies, lost a part of its rationale when we went to a floating exchange rate system.

Q: *When did you leave the White House?*

McCORMACK: I left the White House in 1971. Governor Scranton was my friend. We were both from northern Pennsylvania. I helped him from time to time on presidential projects. The president had asked Scranton to be secretary of state twice and he declined to take the job for various reasons, one of which was he didn't really trust Nixon. He knew that Nixon intended to pull all foreign policy decision-making into the Executive Office and the National Security Council. He did not want to be a figurehead secretary of state. He also had family considerations.

He did, however, agree to help Nixon from time to time with troubleshooting assignments. It was on that basis that he chaired the INTELSAT negotiation. A year later the Scranton Commission on Campus Unrest was set up to deal with the increasing war-related violence on campuses. The Kent State event was a pure anti-war demonstration that got out of hand. Jackson State was a racial issue in which young people were killed by state police. Bill Scranton took this assignment at the request of the president and Ehrlichman. It was a crash project to identify the causes of campus unrest and to offer some suggestions for dealing with them.

Shortly after he took this assignment, Scranton learned that the White House staff had second thoughts about the wisdom of establishing the commission. Our country was experiencing a recession in 1970 and some of the political strategists at the White House decided that they would use campus radicals as the hate object for the fall campaign to distract people from the recession issue. Bill Scranton's Commission on Campus Unrest was thus perceived as a potential problem by the White House because they had created it themselves. So they decided they would force the commission to move out of the White House and into some distant quarters on H Street. The White House intended to distance itself from the commission and ultimately attack it.

Naturally, I had friends in the White House. I had been seconded from the Ash Council for three months to work on this project at the request of Scranton. I had a great personal respect for Scranton, and I obviously felt that when I was working for him I needed to be loyal to him. So I offered my large office in the EOB to the governor for the duration of the Commission on Campus Unrest project. This infuriated some of the White House operatives who were anxious to distance themselves from the commission.

Q: Who at that time do you feel were calling these political shots?

McCORMACK: I forget who they all were, but it was Colson and Clawson and some of Bob Haldeman's people and Ehrlichman. Whatever the case, to make a very long story short, I was coming under increased pressure to force Scranton to move to this building on H Street, where they had pushed everybody else. Scranton felt, for symbolic reasons, it was important for him not to leave the White House complex. He said, "I have done this project at the request of the president." Well, finally toward the end of the summer, the report was nearly finished. Scranton and I went over the draft and toned down some of the negative references to the president and vice president that had been put in the report by the staff. I myself then added part of the preface to the report, which was an admonition to students to remember that they had inherited a considerable legacy from the past and they should not just dissipate it mindlessly. The day that Scranton was to issue his report, the White House had Pat Moynihan schedule an off-the-record press conference at the White House press room to deliver a hatchet job.

Q: He was not then senator?

McCORMACK: No, he was not. He was a domestic policy advisor at the White House. They had Moynihan denounce the report, claiming it was a sellout to the left, was intellectually unsound, and so on. When he learned about Moynihan's actions, Scranton was as angry as I have ever seen him. When he gave his own press conference several hours later, one of the reporters, Izzy Stone, asked, "Do you think there is a failure of moral leadership in this White House?" After a pause, Scranton banged his fist on the podium and said, "That is exactly what I think the problem is. There is a failure of moral leadership in this White House." The press conference was suddenly over.

Scranton walked out of the press room and went back to my office to rest a bit. He then packed his bags and went back to Scranton, Pennsylvania. Shortly after that, as I went through the main gate of the EOB, the guard said, "Mr. McCormack, this pass will no longer be good after today." So I went into my office and I found that everything had been taken out. My desk had been removed. The only thing remaining was the gold carpet and a great heap of papers in the center of the floor.

Q: Obviously this was not done at the presidential level, but it shows the vindictiveness of some people in the system.

McCORMACK: Well, in any case, I obviously left. The man who had actually done this was one of Haldeman's men, whose name was John Brown III. Of course I was crushed to go from a wonderful job at the age of twenty-nine to being thrown out on my ear. I got on a plane and flew to Belgium to visit the former Belgian ambassador and his family. In the center of Brussels there is a famous statue of Manneken Pis, a little boy peeing. I bought a large postcard featuring this statue, sent it to John Brown III, The White House, Washington, D.C., with the message: "Dear John, Thinking of you. Merry Christmas. Dick McCormack."

This postcard arrived, and some of the women who worked in the White House, many of whom were my friends, passed it around to each other, and eventually it got to Rosemary Woods, who showed it to the president. He said, "What is this about?" At the end of the day John Brown III was fired, and I was briefly rehired. Then I got a visit from a new senior White

House official close to Haldeman, saying that the president had ordered that I be brought back, but he didn't think I had much of a future there. I stayed for a brief time.

Q: Did you sense a change in the atmosphere in the White House? It sounds like initially they wanted to do things, but then all of a sudden it turned into a political machine, anything to be reelected.

McCORMACK: It was more complicated than that. You really have to think of the times. Remember we had hundreds of thousands of demonstrators in the streets of Washington, D.C. We actually had army units hidden in the vast basement of the EOB to defend the White House in case of attack from the streets. There were terrorists and young people going around the country, robbing banks and doing crazy things. We had just had mass race riots in the country a few years before. This was an America that was feeling very embattled. To understand what it was like, to understand why this paranoia developed, you need to have lived through those times. You know, everybody naturally wants to think of themselves as the good guys, trying to do the right thing for the country. I am sure that is how the Nixon people viewed themselves. They viewed themselves as being attacked by lefties and Communist sympathizers, and some of them were.

Everything became very personalized then. That was ultimately the fatal flaw in the Nixon presidency, which Nixon himself recognized much later. The truth of the matter is that the political class is never going to agree on everything. But the White House people in those days tended to define their political relationships based upon one or two issues. You were either 100% with them, or you were suspect.

There were literally enemies lists. Some of those on the enemies list supposedly had their taxes investigated. All sorts of other things happened to them. They took people who disagreed with them on a single issue and made them enemies on everything. So when Nixon himself became vulnerable, which happened after Watergate, there was no pity. They went for his throat. President Lyndon Johnson had also done questionable things. If enough powerful people had wished, they could also have gone for his throat. But Speaker John McCormack and others protected him.

This was a lesson that most subsequent presidents have learned. They have made it their business to try to heal the wounds after policy disputes to avoid creating permanent enemies. That was a lesson Nixon learned too late, and it cost him his presidency. In any case, I left Washington in 1971 and went back to my home in Bradford, Pennsylvania.

VENTURES OUTSIDE OF GOVERNMENT

Q: You left Washington when?

McCORMACK: 1971. I went back to my home in Pennsylvania to run for Congress. With no money or staff, I planned to run against the incumbent Republican congressman, Albert W. Johnston. These eleven counties of northern Pennsylvania were in many ways economically depressed. My home county, McKean, had a bit more money than most because of the oil, but Bradford was surrounded by large swaths of Appalachia plus Penn State. There was a net tax drain of a quarter billions dollars every year that went from these poor counties to Washington, D.C. Nationally, a huge amount of money was raised by taxes and recycled by Washington through programs. If your congressman was not active in getting money from these programs, you were simply providing money for other people to spend in other parts of the country. So that was the first big drain on the capital and prosperity of the then 23rd Congressional District.

The second big drain on the capital had to do with local banks that would basically get deposits from the region and then re-cycle the money to Pittsburgh and New York, where returns were higher. So we basically had a capital shortage problem. We needed new industries to replace old dying industries. There were all sorts of things that needed to be done to correct the regional economic weakness. I had done a research project on that subject funded by the Commerce Department before I announced that I was running for Congress. I examined what other areas had done to spark investment and growth, including creating research triangles.

Q: Could you explain what a research triangle is?

McCORMACK: That is where you have universities and businesses and professional operations all working together in places such as North Carolina and what later happened in Center County with Penn State. In any case, I started making speeches on this subject at the Rotary Clubs in the region. Of course when the congressman sensed I was going to run against him, he quickly had the money cut off for my study. By then, though, it was too late for him. I had already raised these issues to such a level that my ideas began to get a lot of local support. I then announced that I was going to run for Congress. The problem was we didn't have any money at all. Some of my old friends from high school, however, soon rallied to my cause. The teachers also supported me.

Q: *This would be in the primary.*

McCORMACK: The primary. That area is Republican. Whoever wins the primary usually wins the general election.

Q: *What was the Republican organization in that area? Was there much of one?*

McCORMACK: There was a Republican organization and it was, of course, largely supporting the incumbent. This party organization had atrophied somewhat over time because it never really had to flex its muscles. It was the incumbent party and it was part of old America. I learned later that some of the county chairmen, who didn't have much respect for my opponent, quietly supported me. I went around knocking on doors from morning till night, day after day, week after week, and month after month. I knew that I would have to run twice, the first time to raise the flag and the second time to actually bring it home. I ran the first time and I got 39% of the vote to the astonishment of everybody. I carried the northern counties of my district, including the incumbent's own county and home town. I ran two years later and got 46% of the vote. (The incumbent, Congressman Albert Johnson, subsequently was involved in a money scandal and lost his seat to a Democrat). After my first congressional race, Watergate happened. The people who were my enemies at the White House were suddenly gone. I was invited to come back to the White House right after the second election and did some research and analysis on OPEC.

Q: *When was this?*

McCORMACK: This was in 1974. I wrote papers on what we could do to counter OPEC. Then when Nixon resigned, Ford came into office. Governor Scranton was one of the important members of his transition. I provided a proposed "spokes in the wheel" White House staff reporting arrangement to prevent any single powerful individual from monopolizing the information channel to the president. My proposal was intensely resented by President Ford's new chief of staff, Don Rumsfeld. But with the memory of the Haldeman system fresh in so many people's minds, my proposal, which was based on the post Sherman Adams Eisenhower White House model, was implemented.

Another important member of his transition was Tom Whitehead, a friend. At this time, I wanted to go to the Treasury Department to continue work on OPEC-related problems. I was made deputy to the assistant secretary of the Treasury, with responsibilities for Saudi Arabian operations. I began flying back and forth to Saudi Arabia to see what we could do about getting as much of our oil money as possible back to the U.S. to avoid a current accounts debacle.

Q: What was the situation in Saudi Arabia vis-a-vis our interests at that point?

McCORMACK: It was, of course, a very complicated situation. In the 1967 War, Israel expanded its borders.

Q: This was known as the Six-Day War?

McCORMACK: Yes. Israel expanded its borders considerably. There were some in Israel who wanted to have that expansion be permanent, which was widely resented in the Arab world. So when an opportunity arose to strike back at Israel with the help of the Russians, a war was organized in 1973 to attack Israel. This attack was an astonishing thing to the Israelis, and for a few days it appeared successful. Were it not for the tactical mistakes of the Syrian Army after their original breakthrough near the Golan Heights, they could have driven on through to Jerusalem and Tel Aviv. But instead the Syrian tank armies just circled around under the Golan Heights for two days. By then we were able to provide Israel with enough new weapons to deal with the military crisis they were facing. The Russians not only provided the Arabs with advice, they also provided them with anti-aircraft missiles and all sorts of other things.

Q: Very effective.

McCORMACK: In any case, you had the 1967 Six-Day War, which was a great success for the Israelis. Then you had the 1973 war, which was a disaster. Eventually the Israelis won, but they suffered terrible losses. The Arabs basically felt that the Americans had helped the Israelis in their hour of need, and they threatened us with an oil embargo unless some kind of settlement between Israel and the Palestinians occurred. They also confiscated the holdings of the American oil companies in Saudi Arabia and elsewhere. We wound up with an enormous problem. So I went to the Treasury to work on this complex of issues.

In those early days, there were three different theories about what to do about soaring oil prices and OPEC. You had one group of strategists from the outside. Ed Luttwak, for example, wanted to go in with military force to seize Arab oil. He and his friends wrote many articles urging this policy. The second option was to do nothing about the increase in the price of oil, which was putting increasing strain on many economies in the world, and simply let one or two major countries go bust. As one man said ironically, "Use the corpse of Italy to flog OPEC into being more reasonable on oil prices." That too was rejected. The third option was to take the oil dollars and recycle them to other countries, using our banks, to prevent the Arabs from directly using the money themselves to extract political leverage.

In the meantime, the plan was to encourage as much oil production as possible in as many different places as possible so as to create a supply and demand situation that would no longer allow OPEC to have the clout on prices that it did. It was the third plan that was eventually launched and implemented.

In the Treasury Department, there was a young assistant secretary close to Secretary Simon who was my direct superior. For various reasons, he and I did not enjoy a warm personal relationship. So I returned to the White House and worked at the trade office on a major commodity policy initiative.

The tension at the Treasury Department did not improve, however, and press leaks documented an ugly series of personnel and policy disputes, spiced by an embarrassing candid camera incident involving the young assistant secretary. Finally a White House ultimatum stopped the leaks by all parties.

Q: Could you explain what the Commodity Policy Initiative was?

McCORMACK: Yes. Henry Kissinger had earlier gone to the United Nations and in a major speech proposed that, just as OPEC has organized its own cartel on oil, there should be similar internationally organized price-fixing cartels for copper, lead, zinc, etc. Fred Bergsten was one of the intellectual authors of this plan in an article entitled "Two, Three, Many OPECs." He reasoned that if supply and demand could be brought into permanent balance, we wouldn't have wide fluctuations in prices. Kissinger proposed this idea to create greater solidarity with the Third World, both for Cold War objectives and to prevent OPEC from isolating the United States. When I was brought to the Trade Office by Ambassador Malmgren to look at this issue, it soon became clear to me that this policy initiative was ill-conceived.

It is extremely difficult to second-guess the market on commodity prices on a long-term basis. You have new mineral deposits that are being discovered constantly. You have technological breakthroughs that make some products obsolete, others in greater demand. You have impoverished countries that suddenly discover a local resource base. Such countries cannot be counted upon to cooperate with a price-fixing cartel, where other countries basically would have a large established share of the global market. Under the Kissinger plan, new entrants would not be allowed to exploit new high quality deposits. So I wrote a 25 or 30-page paper demonstrating what I thought was the impracticality of the Kissinger Initiative. When I showed it to the trade ambassador, he read it and he said, "Oh! Oh!"

Q: Who was that?

McCORMACK: Harold Malmgren. He called in Bob Hormats, who was then an advisor to Kissinger and the National Security Council on economic issues. He too read it and took it to Kissinger. Kissinger read it and didn't say anything except "Call in Tom Enders." [At the time, Tom

Enders was the assistant secretary of state for economics and business, who had coordinated Kissinger's UN speech.] I wasn't present, but Ambassador Malmgren told me what happened at that meeting. It wasn't a pretty scene. Shortly after this happened, Enders resigned to become the new Ambassador to Canada. Enders' assistant, who had actually drafted the earlier Kissinger speech, left government. In any case, U.S. policy was dramatically changed. I was then offered a position at the American Enterprise Institute, which at that time was close to the kitchen cabinet of President Ford, including former Defense Secretary Mel Laird.

Q: OK, you are talking about going to the American Enterprise Institute. So many of these things represent different parts of the political establishment. What was the genesis of this?

McCORMACK: The American Enterprise Institute was a think tank that was set up by a remarkable Lebanese American named Bill Baroody, but in fact in many ways it had become a Mel Laird instrument when President Ford became president. Mel Laird was again very influential because he was an old friend of the President's. So in effect the kitchen cabinet of the Ford presidency was in part staffed by the American Enterprise Institute. I did some of that work myself on different foreign policy issues. At that time, much of the political establishment felt that Kissinger had accumulated too much influence. The American Enterprise Institute, among others, was tasked with creating alternative policy options for the president.

During this period, Kissinger was secretary of state. His able former deputy, General Brent Scowcroft, became the national security advisor. There was a feeling among many Republicans that there were gaps and flaws in some of Kissinger's policies that needed to be addressed. I was part of this effort. From time to time, I also went to New York to help Governor Scranton with his speeches. Scranton was the U.N. Ambassador under President Ford. I also traveled through the Middle East and elsewhere during this time.

Q: What was the feeling about Kissinger? Was it a matter that he had too much power or was off on the wrong course?

McCORMACK: I think the feeling about him was that he was right about ninety percent of the time but on an important ten percent he was wrong, and that his ability to manipulate the system was greater than his ability to provide consistently wise advice across the board. There was also the feeling that he was not always totally candid with his colleagues and peers about what he had been doing and what he was intending to do. There was, therefore, a lack of complete confidence in him in large parts of the political establishment in Washington. This included Mel Laird, who had been the secretary of defense when Kissinger was the national security advisor under Nixon.

I was originally brought to the attention of AEI by the White House when the report I had written on commodity policy proved to be more sound than the speech Kissinger had made earlier to the United Nations. I worked there for several years.

Q: This was when?

McCORMACK: President Ford arrived in 1974, so I was at AEI in 1975, 1976, and part of 1977. When President Ford lost the election to Carter, Bill Baroody decided that the American Enterprise Institute would become the shadow Republican government in exile.

Q: During the election of '76, were there any foreign affairs issues that you got involved in?

McCORMACK: We were actively involved as individuals in the campaign on issues of development and strategy. At one time I actually had a part-time office in Nixon's old suite in the Executive Office of the President.

Q: Were there any issues that you particularly got involved with?

McCORMACK: That was a long time ago. I was involved in writing speeches, tactical responses, numerous foreign affairs issues, and some of the economic issues. However, there was one memorable event that occurred to me during the primary elections. Mel Laird was anxious to support President Ford over his challenger Ronald Reagan. One day I received a call from one of Reagan's speechwriters. He said, "Dick, I know you are supporting Ford, but you have been a friend of mine for a long time. I have a personal favor to ask. Governor Reagan is going to be making a speech in Philadelphia on Tuesday before the World Affairs Council on the problems of the Third World. The person who is in charge of doing that speech has just handed me his draft." This was on Friday. Then he said, "This draft is utterly unusable. Could I ask you as a personal favor to write a speech on the problems of the Third World over the weekend?" I said, "Yes. As long as you don't embarrass me."

I took papers I had been writing on various Third World problems and put them together in the form of a speech, and I had it hand-carried to my friend that Sunday night. He read it and said that it was perfect, "I am not going to change a single word." So he gave it to Governor Reagan, and the governor apparently liked it. He went to the Philadelphia World Affairs Council and read the speech. But seven or eight times in the course of that speech where I had written the words "Third World," Governor Reagan said: "the Third World War." Unfortunately for everybody, Bob Novak, the journalist, was in the audience.

Q: He was a columnist.

McCORMACK: Yes, and he counted them. He wrote a savage article about the repeated slip. But of course it raised questions in my mind about Governor Reagan.

Ford lost that election very narrowly. He lost it for several reasons. He lost it because Arthur Burns at the Federal Reserve cut it too fine and held a tight monetary policy for too long. The politically sensitive numbers on the U.S. economy only turned around in December, a month after Ford had lost the election. Greenspan did the same thing to President G. H. W. Bush with similar consequences in 1992.

Q: Bush one.

McCORMACK: Yes. So that was the first and most important problem that occurred. A final problem happened at the very end of the campaign. Ford's polls were rising and Carter's were falling. Then a disruptive visit by a black activist to the church of Jimmy Carter, the Clendenon King incident, occurred. This was portrayed by the Carter people as an attempt by Republican activists to embarrass Jimmy Carter in his own white church. It was just enough in the South to tilt the election in the other direction.

No one was ever able to prove that King was in fact an agent of the Democrats' campaign, but King's brother was reported in the press to have previously received money from the Carter campaign to divert votes from a white liberal competitor when Carter was running earlier for governor of Georgia. So I assumed that this was a staged event. This happened on the Sunday before the election on Tuesday, and I couldn't get anybody on the campaign to focus fast enough to be able to at least raise the question effectively as to whether this was a Democratic plot instead of a Republican dirty tricks event to embarrass Jimmy Carter in his church, as it was portrayed throughout the South. Post-election polls showed that this was just enough of an embarrassment to tilt the balance to Jimmy Carter.

After the presidential election of 1976 was over, William Baroody made far-reaching changes in the American Enterprise Institute. The neoconservative forces were invited in and gradually took over AEI. On his deathbed shortly thereafter, Baroody told some of his closest associates that his succession plan for AEI was the greatest mistake of his life. But by then, the die was cast.

I left and did private consulting for a couple of years with my old boss, Walter Thayer, and others in New York.

Q: When you say private consulting, what does this really mean?

McCORMACK: People give you a problem and say, "Help us solve this." For example, I received a call from one of my business clients a couple days ago saying that they were having difficulties getting a certain block of stock registered in Brazil. They were concerned that this was the result of questionable activities on the part of the people who wanted to benefit another investor, a local investor. So they asked me whether I could arrange to go to Brazil and appeal to the central bank to help this American company obtain fair registration of their stock. They also wanted me to find out what was blocking this registration. Other projects involved vetting potential joint venture partners to learn if these people had a good reputation. If there was a possible question of bribery, sometimes I would talk to the American ambassadors.

Another kind of consulting involves macroeconomic analyses. If a country is booming, then a cellular telephone license is worth a lot of money. If the economy is at its peak and is about to weaken, that license isn't worth as much in the short term. Sometimes you will have outrageous situations where a government simply has ripped off foreign investors. Then I quietly arrange to see certain foreign government officials. Since these governments know that I have a reputation for being honest, if I start going around saying there is a big problem in country X, other investors may not be as quick to invest.

I have a pretty good record of getting things done for people when they have a legitimate case. I won't take a client that I feel is doing something that I am not comfortable with. I also decline to take countries as clients. I have turned down huge retainers from some countries. Of course my former colleagues in the State Department know this. So whenever I need some help or advice overseas from my former colleagues, it is almost always forthcoming.

As I travel around the world, I sometimes see problems that I think might need more attention by our own government. Then I write pro bono policy analyses that go to the State Department, White House, Treasury Department, and Congress. I have done this sort of thing for a very long time. Gradually over the years, doors opened all over the world. There is almost no country I visit where I can't see whomever I want to see today and expect reasonable candor.

Q: You were doing this consulting after you left the American Enterprise Institute?

McCORMACK: I did it from 1977 to 1978, and then in 1979 I went to work for Senator Helms on the Foreign Relations Committee.

SENATOR HELMS AND THE
FOREIGN RELATIONS COMMITTEE

Q: You were with Helms from when to when?

McCORMACK: From 1979 to 1981.

Q: How did that come about?

McCORMACK: I was approached by one of the senator's staffers, who had seen some of the policy analyses I had just written on the Camp David Accords and on Soviet political and economic warfare. These papers were also widely circulated at the State Department and the NSC. Our allies were under attack all over the Third World. Problems in Afghanistan were developing. I pulled the whole picture together and wrote a 40-page paper called "Soviet Political and Economic Warfare: Challenge and Response." I had it privately printed and distributed to all the members of the Trilateral Commission at their spring meeting in 1978.

Q: You might explain what the Trilateral Commission is.

McCORMACK: In 1973 David Rockefeller asked Zbigniew Brzezinski to form an organization of top political and business leaders from Japan, Europe, and North America. This organization was called the Trilateral Commission and it was set up to foster closer political and economic cooperation in addressing the problems facing the three regions. I was not a member of this commission, but I had friends who were and they helped me distribute this report. In any case, this report was also circulated on the Hill.

I also had written a paper on the plusses and minuses of the Camp David Accords. After these two papers were circulated, one of Senator Helms's staffers approached me to ask if I would consider giving advice to the senator whom I had never met. I had a good subsequent relationship with the senator. He treated me well. At that time, I had just been offered a more senior position by another prominent senator, but I discovered that the other senator had a reputation for treating staff badly.

Q: We are talking about 1979. What was the position of Senator Helms in the Senate, and what was his reputation? He was sort of a bete noire to the State Department. How did you feel about it?

McCORMACK: What I had heard about Senator Helms before I took the job was that he was more conservative on some issues than I was, and that was certainly true, but also that he was a person of integrity who treated his staff in a dignified way. Senator Helms was a man who was actively committed to his faith. People who sometimes did the most outrageous things would come and simply ask for his forgiveness, and he would almost always forgive them. It is important to understand the two sides of Senator Helms. Everybody understands the right-wing side. What they don't understand is the other side, and there is another side. For example, the Clinton White House decided that they would hire a few Republicans for ambassadorships after the 1996 elections. They offered the Mexican ambassadorship to Governor Weld of Massachusetts.

As it happened, Governor Weld had attacked Senator Helms in one of his campaigns in a highly personal way. The Mexicans were anxious to have Governor Weld come to Mexico. They knew he was active and had many friends. So a Mexican diplomat came to me and said, "We know that you earlier worked with Senator Helms. He is blocking Governor Weld. What can be done to deal with this?" I said to him, "All Governor Weld has to do is go into Senator Helms's office, close the door, and offer a personal apology." I said, "If the Governor does this, the Senator will almost certainly forgive him. He will be the next ambassador to Mexico. If he will not apologize, not only will Weld not be the next ambassador to Mexico, you don't want him as your ambassador." He would not apologize, and Helms blocked him.

There also were astonishing cases involving Foreign Service officers who had been involved in things they shouldn't have. The security people in the State Department occasionally secretly sent documentation on chronic compromising behavior to Senator Helms because they were concerned such people could be blackmailed. When such individuals came and appealed to the Senator, admitted their mistakes, and pledged never to do them again, the person was almost always forgiven by Helms, confirmed, and sent to his next post. The point I want to make is this: Helms was very tough. He had very strong principles. He had a hard line view toward the Soviet Union, which I felt was appropriate at the time I was working with him. Those were views that ultimately prevailed in the Reagan administration. But the people on his staff at the time, with the exception of one man whom I didn't like very much, were very decent people.

Q: There are two people whose names I can't recall, but come up in interviews. One was, I think, a retired rear admiral.

McCORMACK: Yes, Bud Nance, a fine gentleman.

Q: He was considered to be a difficult person. The other was a woman who was supposedly very instrumental in South American policy in support of dictators.

McCORMACK: That was Debbie De Moss. She came on the staff after I left. Admiral Bud Nance had been the number two in the policy planning section of the Joint Chiefs of Staff. He later served as the deputy national security advisor at one point under Reagan. In 1992, Senator Helms was ill. He had back problems, a heart problem, and was worn down. There was dissension on the staff, and the ill and aging senator wasn't able to cope with it. He asked his old friend, the admiral, to come back to take over the staff. So he did, but he only accepted a dollar a year in compensation.

Unfortunately, Admiral Nance went to North Korea as part of a delegation that included General Stilwell and Joe Churba to talk about U.S. missing in action soldiers from the Korean War. When they returned, within a year, three of the four were dead with diseases that they had not had before. Nance came down with a mysterious illness that no one could trace. He lingered year after year, sometimes under the most appalling circumstances, requiring weekly transfusions. The admiral believed he and his earlier traveling companions had been targets of a North Korean intelligence operation to kill them in a way that couldn't be traced, by the use of poisons or germs. I have no idea whether that is true or not, but that is what the admiral believed. He actually asked me to report this to friends of mine in the CIA to determine if a recent defector couldn't be interrogated to learn whether medical pathogens were being used by North Korea's intelligence service.

I first knew Bud Nance in 1980, when he came to the staff to work on the SALT Treaty issues. He had just come out of the Pentagon. He was very well briefed on all the details. He did a very professional job for the senator during that period. Then he became the deputy national security advisor at the White House. He was a gentleman.

Q: Did you get any feel for the senator's policy towards Latin America? Reagan came in around the time you were there and he seemed to be a great supporter of what we call the right-wing dictatorships.

McCORMACK: 1980 was the height of the Cold War. You had active Cuban and Russian attempts to destabilize and communize Central America. When I was on the senator's staff, I went to Nicaragua in 1980. I got to know many of the Sandinista leaders, including Borge and Ortega. The message I had for them was this: "We don't particularly like the government of Mr. Tito in Yugoslavia. We know he runs an authoritarian regime. If you refrain from exporting your revolution and treat your own people halfway decently, you, like Tito, will not have problems with the U.S. government. But if you start exporting guns and revolution to the neighborhood, we will be on you like a frog on a June bug."

They assured me that they would not export revolution and guns or attempt to subvert the region. But in fact they did. The rest is history. The Third World counterattacks by the Reagan administration and other measures increased the cost to the Soviet Union. Eventually the Soviet Union's economy cracked under financial pressure. The defeat in Afghanistan in particular also helped break the morale of the muscular side of the Soviet security services.

Q: From 1979 to 1981 was an important time because you had two major developments at the end of 1979. One was the Iranian revolution—the taking of our embassy in Tehran, and also the Soviet invasion of Afghanistan, which

*was, as you say, a major factor in the eventual dissolution of the Soviet empire.
How was this viewed from Helms's point of view, and what were you doing?*

McCORMACK: I had nothing to do with what was going on in Iran at the
time, except for the odd speech and analysis. I had, however, been working
on that issue before I came to Helms's office as part of my normal activity.
I had been doing analytical work on that problem, which went through
a senior White House official named Sam Hoskinson at the National
Security Council. Sam had been sent to the NSC by CIA Director George
Bush and was kept on after Carter won the election. I often sent copies of
my analyses to Hoskinson, which I did *pro bono*. So I did a lot of analytical
work on Khomeini, what he was doing, and where he might go.

At that time, George Ball took a very hopeful view towards Khomeini. He
used to describe him to Carter and Cyrus Vance as "just a conservative
religious leader." George was a heavyweight in the American foreign policy
establishment of the time. My view was different. I felt that there were
going to be terrible problems with Khomeini in power. I thought that we
should have been more supportive of the shah.

In my analysis, I described how I thought Khomeini would consolidate power
once he had his foot in the door. Events unfolded exactly as I had predicted.
In the end, Brzezinski became convinced, according to Sam, of the dangers
of Khomeini, but by then it was too late. It would have taken a considerable
effort, and Secretary of State Vance was utterly opposed to it. Toward the end
of the shah's rule, there was a little flurry of effort by the Carter administration
to stabilize the Iranian situation, but by then it was far too late. You had the
additional potential problem in Iran of the underground Communist Tudeh
Party, which was a rather big operation at one time.

*Q: Well, when you were on Helms's staff, 1979 to 1981, how were relations
with the Department of State? Later that became sort of septic.*

McCORMACK: They were terrible.

Q: At that time?

McCORMACK: Senator Helms was pushing his foreign policy views. It is
important to keep this in perspective. If you take the conservative Republican

view and then take the State Department view of 1980, they would overlap in about eighty percent of the cases. Both sides would probably deny that, but that is really true. It was 20 percent of the issues where there was a lot of neuralgia and where honest people could differ over ways of playing the chess game. Once you are in the middle of your chess game strategy, it is hard to shift. That, by the way, is the great value of our four-year elections, because it allows the country to disengage itself from mistakes.

In the case of the Helms operation, one of the issues that I worked on was Rhodesia. My PhD dissertation addressed racial issues in East Africa. My articulated view on race issues is that we need to come together to work on the basis of merit. I was not in favor of Mugabe, however, a man I knew to be bitter and deeply flawed. I thought he would be a disaster in power, which proved to be the case. I monitored the elections that took place in that country in 1979 and 1980. I would often stop by before my trips to see Jerry Funk, the able National Security Council director for Africa, and sometimes Dick Moose, the assistant secretary of state for Africa. We had very candid discussions. At that time, Senator Helms was supporting Bishop Muzorewa, who was a moderate black leader.

The British had a different strategy. They basically hoped in the end that there would be a stalemate between Nkomo, who was the Soviet-supported Matabele leader, Mugabe, who was the China-sponsored Shona leader, moderate Bishop Muzorewa, another Shona leader who had South African support, and Ian Smith, who was the white leader. The British hoped that the elections could be so organized that no faction would get an absolute majority. Any subsequent government would thus, they reasoned, have to form coalitions, and all people would be protected by this balance of power. But the British authorities allowed Mugabe's guerrilla forces to intimidate the tribal trust areas during a crucial election. It was a ruthless intimidation, which caused the people to vote overwhelmingly for Mugabe rather than Muzorewa.

For example, I went to one guerrilla encampment on the day of the 1980 elections and saw a whole corral full of young girls about twelve or thirteen years old dressed in beautiful Sunday clothes. I learned that these were youngsters who had been kidnapped from the surrounding areas by Mugabe's guerrillas. Local parents were told that if Mugabe won the election, the children would be allowed to return home. But if Mugabe lost the election, these children would be seized, turned into porters for the revolution, and then taken into Mozambique. I actually saw the children myself. They were like frightened little quail. That kind of intimidation in different forms was occurring all over the Shona areas of Rhodesia. Of course parents wanted their children back, and they voted for Mugabe. So Mugabe won an absolute majority.

The British authorities were utterly shocked by the unexpected lopsided election results. But it was too late. Mugabe as president has proved to be a terrible long-term curse to his country's people. Inflation has soared. Living standards have collapsed. Life expectancy has fallen by fifty percent. Human rights have vanished. The election of Mugabe poisoned an entire nation for a generation.

There were two types of leaders in Africa who suffered under the colonial and white rule. One type was like Mandela, who transcended the evil that had been inflicted on him and became a real blessing to his country. Like Mandela, Mugabe also suffered. He was jailed by Ian Smith and treated badly. He emerged deeply embittered.

When you make policy judgments, you have to understand the people you are dealing with. You need to be able to make judgments about what these people will be like if they get into power. After traveling around Zimbabwe and the region in 1979 and 1980, I concluded that Mugabe was going to be truly bad news for everybody in the country if he came into power. I did everything I could to block him.

Q: When you say you did what you could, basically this was having to convince Helms?

McCORMACK: Yes, and then getting blocs of senators to support the first election that Muzorewa won. We had a lot of support in the House and Senate. I wrote articles that appeared in the press, some under my own name, some under the senator's, describing what was going on and predicting what would happen if Mugabe were allowed to take power. This is a long and detailed story that we don't have time to go into today. It represents a little country. It depresses me to see how one ruthless and bitter person can take a prosperous country and really trash it. That is what Mugabe has done to Zimbabwe.

Q: Unfortunately, we are seeing a good number of countries like that. How did you find Senator Helms's relations and influence in the Foreign Relations Committee and in the Senate at this time?

McCORMACK: He was never a member of the club, nor did he want to be. He had a very strong national constituency of people who thought like him. They were the ones who funded his campaigns with small contributions. Part of his strength was the fact that he would insist upon senators actually standing up, voting on sensitive issues, and going on record. Some senators were reluctant to do that because it would antagonize this bloc or that bloc of voters.

Part of the basis of Helms's strength was that he forced his colleagues to go on record. A second part of his strength was that he really didn't care what the Senate and the broader establishment thought of him. He really didn't. At the time I lived at the Watergate, and he urged me to leave because he felt that all my establishment neighbors and friends there would somehow influence my behavior and my policy thinking. The point is that he didn't care what *The New York Times* wrote about him. What he cared about was what people of his background in his state and across the nation thought of him. He viewed himself as their representative.

Helms was also a very underestimated man. He worked hard to master the briefs. He fought hard on personnel and policies. He once said, "There is no point in just making a speech if you are not willing to fight for it, because then all you have done is taken a symbolic position." If he thought that someone was the wrong person for a federal position, he would occasionally try to block that person. One of the staff occasionally targeted people unfairly, which I would then seek to remedy with the facts.

Q: Did you get the feeling that the ability to stop appointments is quite a bit of power in the Washington game? If you have a senator who is willing to use this sort of power on your recommendation, this could be pretty nasty stuff.

McCORMACK: Remember, in those days, the stakes were high and there were strong feelings on strategy. We did have one person on the staff who was on a power trip. But he was no more ruthless toward the State Department than he was toward his own staff colleagues who sometimes disagreed with him. Senator Helms took seriously his constitutional Senate role of advice and consent. The senator also worked hard to support people he believed would help the country. He supported me for a position in the Reagan administration. I had applied to be director of intelligence and research in the State Department. Eventually, Under Secretary Dick Kennedy asked me if I would become the assistant secretary for economics, since I had previous White House and Treasury economics experience. Later I became OAS ambassador and under secretary of state for economics. But in all those years I was at the State Department, Helms only called me twice to ask for a favor. He told his staff that he did not want to put me in a compromising position in the Department of State. One request was to help get landing rights for Lufthansa in Charlotte, North Carolina. Another was a tobacco-related issue. Because my father had just died of throat cancer brought on by smoking, I declined to help on that issue. But those are the only two times he ever called me and asked for anything.

Q: Before we finish the Helms discussion, did you run across Jeane Kirkpatrick at that point?

McCORMACK: Yes, occasionally. There were some similarities between her famous *Commentary* essay and my earlier 1978 paper on Soviet political and economic warfare, which I had submitted in draft to *Commentary* magazine for possible publication. She later did a great job at the United Nations for the Reagan administration

Former President Nixon, however, eventually took my paper, which appeared as the cover story of *Army Magazine* in February 1979, and quoted me at length in his book *The Real War*. So my thesis got pretty wide circulation. The Reagan administration implemented almost all of my policy recommendations. Some of the predictions I made about what would happen to the Soviet Union if in fact they ever engaged in real detente and liberalization, actually unfolded with dramatic consequences under Gorbachev. I will give you a copy of my article, and you can draw your own conclusions.

BUSINESS AND ECONOMICS
AT STATE

Q: In 1981 you went to the Department of State. How did you get the job?

McCORMACK: During the course of the transition, I applied through the normal political process of the White House to be the Director of Intelligence and Research at the State Department. I was supported in this by Ted Shackley [the legendary former deputy director for operations at CIA], former President Nixon, Senator Lugar, Senator Durenberger, and Senator Helms, who I was working with, and quite a large number of other people. This process dragged on and on, and finally the White House sent a direct order to the State Department to put me on as a consultant pending the formal appointment. I then received a call from Dick Kennedy, the under secretary for management, who had known me from previous incarnations at the White House.

Q: He was also Haig's right-hand administrative man.

McCORMACK: He was Al Haig's closest confidante, and a man of immense integrity and ability.

Q: I have interviewed him.

McCORMACK: He said to me that he thought that I would be a fine addition to the Department, but he said, "I am going to suggest to the Secretary that we make you Assistant Secretary for Economics and Business Affairs [EB] rather than the Intelligence and Research director." He reported that the incumbent, Bob Hormats, was probably going to be promoted to be the under secretary of state for economic affairs, and I would then fill Bob's position. So I said, "Fine." I was then made a consultant in the EB front office.

Bob Hormats and I had known each other from the past and we got along well. I attended all of his staff meetings. I naturally never said anything, just attended and watched how Bob handled many issues. This went on for several months. I went to Japan at one point, and spent three weeks there looking at the Japanese economy. I traveled all through the country from the northern islands to the southern tip, looking at all aspects of the economy with the enthusiastic support of Ambassador Mike Mansfield.

Q: What was your impression of the Japanese economy? Where did it stand then and what were your feelings about its strengths and weaknesses. What were you getting from our embassy and other people at that time, 1981?

McCORMACK: As you know, I am a PhD historian. I had read extensively about Japan, its past, its culture, and its civilization. I was also aware of the multiple trade problems that we had. Bob Hormats at that time was trying to arrange for a voluntary restraint agreement on automobiles. The flood of cars into the country was beginning to put pressure on Detroit. The dollar was very strong, and this helped Japanese sales here. There was a lot of concern in Congress about this. In any case, I went to Japan and traveled around the country.

While I was in Japan, I had the first of many interesting conversations with Tomashiko Ushiba, the former chief assistant to the late Prince Konoye. Konoye was the Premier of Japan in the months before the Pearl Harbor attack. He was a man from a distinguished, traditional family. I had learned of the existence of his former chief assistant, Tomashiko Ushiba, from John Toland's book: The Rising Sun. While I was in Japan, I asked the U.S. Embassy if this man were still alive and if they could arrange for me to meet him as part of my orientation exercise. It turned out that Ushiba was living in retirement in North Kamikura, a very elegant suburb of Tokyo.

So I visited the old gentleman, a Cambridge-educated retired banker, dressed in elegant tweeds. He lived in a Swedish type bungalow with his wife. This was the first of a half dozen long meetings I had with this man over the next several years. To my initial astonishment, he turned out to be the elder brother of the former Ambassador to Washington Ushiba, whom I knew from meetings during the Nixon Administration. Konoye's former assistant told me at length about events in 1941 and later. He stated that before Pearl Harbor, Konoye with the support of the Emperor had made a final effort to prevent a war with the United States. He had sent a letter to Roosevelt asking him to meet in Hawaii. He intended to announce a new policy in Hawaii immediately after the Roosevelt meeting. His intention, according to Ushiba, was to accommodate the U.S. demands on China. Konoye knew he would be assassinated when he returned to Japan after the Roosevelt meeting, but the order to withdraw Japanese troops from China would be executed immediately by a prearranged Imperial command and war with the U.S. avoided. Unfortunately, for whatever reason Roosevelt declined to meet with Konoye, and the rest is history.

After the war was over, according to Ushiba, MacArthur called Konoye in and said that he wanted to work with him to build a new Japan. He said that he was aware of his earlier efforts to prevent the war, and he had read of his broader vision for Japan. He asked if Konoye would cooperate with him in doing this. Konoye agreed. So he came back from the meeting with MacArthur, met with Ushiba, and pulled together a remnant of their old staff. They began working on reconstruction plans. However, Konoye never heard back from MacArthur. Ushiba assumed that Washington had vetoed MacArthur's proposal. A month after the MacArthur-Konoye meeting, Konoye's name was printed in the newspaper as a class-A war criminal, among a long list of other accused class-A war criminals. Konoye committed suicide after reading this article.

When I returned to the department after that trip, I went to the State Department library, and I found the manuscript of Konoye's diary, which described his views, his interests, and his general perspective. Konoye, of course, remains a controversial man. I have subsequently met other members of his distinguished family on trips to Japan.

But to get back to your main question about the economy of the country, what I saw in Japan at that time was a modernizing, automating, industrial behemoth that was obviously moving in one direction rapidly, and that was up. It was very clear to me that in the U.S., the quality of U.S. cars had deteriorated, that they had not kept up the pace of innovation that was characteristic of the U.S. industry in the '50s and '40s and '30s. They had rested on their laurels and created a quality vacuum in the U.S. economic system that could be exploited. The over-valued dollar turned a competitive trickle into a flood of imports.

Q: The Japanese had created the niche.

McCORMACK: The currency problems, labor legacy costs, and inadequacies of the American automobile industry itself had created the niche. GM leadership would never have allowed this to happen in the '50s and the '40s and '30s. They produced cutting edge cars. In any case, they had a period where they were a little bit complacent and felt they had a captive market. They allowed the unions to extract excessive benefits. Their problems were complicated by the fact that Japan had what we now call an undervalued currency. I could see what was coming in spades. When I was in Japan for that first trip, I met with one of the leaders of the automobile industry in Japan. He was concerned about pressure building in the U.S. for car import quotas.

On that trip, I met with many other people in Japan: fishermen in Hokkaido, farmer groups in Kyushu, and the most modern parts of their computer companies. Then I came back to the U.S.

Q: Were you picking up two points? One was the restrictive nature of the import controls into Japan, and the other one was the thing that brought them down—the overly close bank loaning system with industry and others, which eventually meant really bad loans.

McCORMACK: This latter aspect was unknown to all of us. The truth of the matter is, the American government never really understood in detail the full complexities of how the Japanese economic system operated until we had the Structural Impediment Initiative in 1989. We understood just how the *keiretsu* operated toward the end of my time in the Department, and that we were in fact dealing with a hybrid economy of Soviet style *Gosplan* plus state capitalism.

Q: You are referring to the Soviet . . .

McCORMACK: The Japanese economy was, in fact, a combination of Albert Speer's German wartime economic plan plus elements of the Soviet *Gosplan*. They took the best elements from their perspective out of each and built a system of state capitalism with a central planning dimension. They, of course, organized industrial espionage operations worldwide to get the best technology they could. They built a vast and very effective lobbying operation here in Washington.

When I left my job as Under Secretary of State, I was by that time certainly one of the two or three top U.S. government experts on Japan's economy. I went to a think tank at the Woodrow Wilson Center. I hadn't been there for three weeks when a gentleman from one of the Japanese companies came, introduced himself to me, and said how much they valued my wisdom. They wanted to employ me as a consultant and asked me if a retainer of $300,000 a year would be fine. I responded that I really didn't want to do that, since I had been working on Japan within the U.S. government all these years. I wasn't comfortable about going out and working for them. Then he said, "$600,000 a year." I told him I didn't think it was appropriate.

The point I want to make is that they hired many former American officials who had some working knowledge of Japan. These people became consultants and advisors or what they called "pipelines" into our system. They built quite a remarkable information-gathering network in Washington. In 1984, a small group of government officials met under the aegis of the vice president every two weeks to talk about the Japanese juggernaut. In one of the meetings, one of my colleagues made a joke about a local Japanese diplomat. Half an hour after the meeting was over, the diplomat called the official who made the joke about him to complain. Now think about that. I only mention this to indicate the full degree to which we were penetrated. There were no secrets in the American government having to do with Japan, none.

It was believed that some people would come into our system and get involved with these issues with the hope of going out and cashing in. That was not true of most people, but there were some who actually did this. Unfortunately, that was not just true of Japan. Other parts of the world have interests in the decisions that are made in the capital of the most powerful country in the world. Fortunately, the vast majority of people who are working in our government are honorable and totally interested in only one thing, which is the welfare of the United States in its broadest sense. Eventually, however, legislation and executive orders were enacted to make this revolving door process more difficult. It had become an open scandal.

Q: When you started in the State Department, was there a Mr. or Mrs. Japanese economy within INR or on the desk or within your bureau?

McCORMACK: The political reporting was better by far than the economic reporting. You had officers who had spent time in Japan. Phil Trezise, who had previously been the Assistant Secretary for Economics, was certainly one of the great repositories of information about Japan, but he had retired to the Brookings Institution long before. There was a cadre of people in the department who did have experience with Japan, but their formative years in dealing with Japan had been with a Japan that was prostrate. The entire effort of the American government was to try to help that country get back on its feet.

Many U.S. diplomats developed a tremendous sense of protectiveness about Japan. As this young child that they helped bring up became an adult, it became a formidable power. I don't believe that everybody was psychologically able to make the changes necessary to deal with that adult, which suddenly became a very major presence in the global economy, operating with a very undervalued currency, just as China does today, and cutting huge holes in the American economy. There were, of course, a number of younger people engaged in this process who didn't have that same background and were more open to dealing with the present Japan, rather than the Japan that they had met when it was a bombed-out shell after the Second World War.

Q: Was anybody writing about Japan at that time? One always thinks of The American Challenge *by Servan-Schreiber.*

McCORMACK: "Le Defí Americain"

Q: Was anybody writing "Le Defi Japonais"?

McCORMACK: Not then, but soon books started appearing by some revisionists. *Japan as Number One* by Ezra Vogel came much later.

Q: Did you come into the Department and say, "Boy! We have got a real problem."

McCORMACK: No, but I certainly did not forget what I had learned. We had a longtime military alliance with the Japanese, and we had areas where we cooperated politically. We also had growing trade frictions. The challenge we always faced in dealing with that situation was to maintain a positive political relationship while dealing with the trade frictions. What the Japanese, of course, tried to do was to use the political dimension of the relationship as an umbrella to sort of cover a very one-sided trading policy. They protected their domestic market including a host of non-tariff barriers, and exported abroad like crazy. So this was the challenge.

I developed tremendous personal and professional respect for the Japanese when I got to know them. I also developed great respect for their abilities as trade negotiators. I also discovered that no matter how many trips you made over there, you almost never got a fundamental change in the practice that you were trying to deal with unless you were in a position where you could more or less impose it. That is a crude expression. The point I want to make is that you would go over there, have a wonderful sushi dinner; and get the gold carpet treatment, but when it came right down to the bottom line about getting an opening of the Japanese market, it was extremely difficult to make any progress.

This became well known in the American government to the point that later Secretary Baker simply would not visit Japan. Throughout the time he was Secretary of State, I believe he went to Japan only once or twice, and that was in connection with the Gulf War. Many other people in Congress realized that we were not making any progress in opening up the Japanese market. This produced new trade legislation and led to Super 301 processes and various other means to coerce the Japanese to open their market. That is telescoping a very long process to a very short time.

Q: *Cars always come to mind, but there are two other areas, and those are foodstuffs and textiles. Nixon felt that textiles were part of his political southern strategy.*

McCORMACK: Yes, but understand why Nixon did this. Nixon ran against Jack Kennedy in 1960. The textile interests came to Nixon in 1960 and said, "We actually like you better than we like Kennedy, but we do want some protection for our textile workers down here because we are getting a lot of competition from Japan. We want restrictive legislation passed. Will you support restrictive legislation?" He said, "I will think about it." The textile interests then went to Jack Kennedy and made a similar request. Jack Kennedy said yes to them. The weekend before the 1960 election, pink slips were issued throughout the textile industry to workers warning them they were going to lose their jobs because Nixon was probably going to win the election and would not protect their jobs. Of course what happened was all those textile workers voted *en masse* for somebody they normally wouldn't have voted for, namely a Catholic Yankee, because they wanted to save their jobs. Nixon never forgot this. When the textile people came around to see him eight years later, when he was running again for office, he said, "Where do I sign?"

Q: But by that time, I am going back to '81, you might say the textile thing had reached a stasis or something like that.

McCORMACK: It never reaches a stasis. It is an industry that was viewed by many as a sacrificial lamb for getting trade openings in other areas for the U.S. economy. They were constantly being nipped away during one trade negotiation after another. This has been a steady process that continues to this day. They are basically fighting a rear-guard battle while trying to modernize and automate as much as they can, and by trying to get legislation that protects them.

The point I want to make is that they have fought a rear guard battle for a very long time. The fact that there were so many jobs linked to the textile industry allowed them to fight this rear guard battle. People will vote against you if you are threatening to take away their jobs. This is something that U.S. trade negotiators occasionally forget. Politicians that forget this are sometimes . . .

Q: They are eliminated.

McCORMACK: They become statesmen and former politicians. But anyway right now for example, you see that textiles have again become a key issue in the current trade round. This has naturally caused consternation in the textile industry. The fact is, however, we cannot compete with Asian wages in most textile manufacturing. The global textile competition is utterly cut-throat—consumers benefit.

Q: What was your impression of our embassy in Japan? I am talking about professional staff, dealing with things that you were going to be dealing with.

McCORMACK: My impression was that they were a high quality group of people, particularly the younger officers. I had two young officers who served as my interpreters for this three-week period. They were as bright, capable, and dedicated as you will ever meet. Mansfield himself was a gentleman of great integrity and tremendous prestige. He worked hard to develop a good relationship with the Japanese. He was very protective of Japan, and I think he was a little troubled when I first arrived on the scene, believing that I was going to come with some enormous protectionist agenda and that I didn't have much interest in the Japanese relationship *per se.*

It is absolutely true that I have felt all my professional life that we need to maintain a more balanced opportunity for trade. We needed to open up other markets. I felt that we should not ignore the kind of *de facto* protectionism that we faced in so many different parts of the world. I also was fully cognizant of the overriding importance of the overall political relationship, particularly during the Cold War. I would have leaned somewhat harder on the Japanese to open their economy quicker and allow more rapid currency adjustments if I had had my druthers. After the financial system in Japan cracked in 1990, my priorities totally shifted to try to help prevent a complete financial and political collapse of a key ally.

Q: After your trip to Japan, why were you sitting around listening in meetings and not being confirmed? What was the problem?

McCORMACK: For some months I was a consultant. I had not been formally put forth as an assistant secretary because Bob Hormats was still the assistant secretary. The person he was going to replace as under secretary, Mike Rashish, wanted to stay. Secretary of State Haig wanted him out. The relationship between Rashish and Haig was terrible. So what was supposed to have been a rather brief transition of serving as a consultant lengthened.

Q: Where was Rashish's strength?

McCORMACK: He was close to Richard Perle and the neoconservative networks. He was also one of the people who helped set up the original White House Trade Office for Jack Kennedy.

Q: But his strength would have to have been in the Republican ranks somewhere?

McCORMACK: He was what we would call today a neoconservative, a former Democrat who became involved in the Reagan campaign. He and Haig, however, did not get along very well. They had different views on some issues, and Haig simply didn't like him. Eventually, however, Haig got into a conflict with the White House over Israel's Lebanon campaign and other issues. President Reagan demanded his resignation and fired him when it did not arrive promptly. Suddenly in came George Shultz, whom I did not know. George Shultz brought with him a group of his oldest and closest friends, including Alan Wallace, whom he named under secretary for economic affairs; Ken Dam was named deputy secretary of state, and Van Gorkom became under secretary for management.

A couple of days after he came to the State Department, Shultz called me and said that he had talked to some people about me and that he heard that I was a highly competent professional. But he said, "I want you to meet with Alan Wallace before we make a final decision on whether we proceed further with your appointment." I said, "I would be happy to do that." So Alan Wallace and I had dinner at the Cosmos Club. It was very clear to me that Alan Wallace was a man of immense experience. He had served on the Council of Economic Advisors for President Eisenhower. He was the man who originally had brought George Shultz to the University of Chicago many years earlier. The connection between Alan Wallace and George Shultz appeared to be almost a father-son relationship. In any case, Alan and I talked for several hours that evening, and we discovered that we both admired Eisenhower and that we liked each other. Alan was a very distinguished statistician.

There are two things I will always remember about Alan. One was that he taught me to look carefully and see what the numbers actually said. You would think that would be an automatic thing, but a lot of times when you hear stories and look at the numbers they don't confirm what the story says. Also, sometimes the numbers are wrong, misleading, or incomplete. The second thing I will always remember about Alan Wallace was his immense personal integrity. Alan was essentially a laissez-faire economist. Later as we worked through issues, we agreed on most things.

We occasionally had disagreements over such things as Alan's wish to eliminate the International Coffee Agreement, which was established to stabilize coffee prices at a time we were fighting a war in Central America. I understood his argument, where he said he could save ten cents for every cup of coffee for the American consumer. However, I felt that if we eliminated the coffee agreement, and prices went through the floor, it would imperil a broader objective to stabilize Central America.

I felt that we would lose a lot of political support in Central America for some of our policies, which were already controversial. I strongly disagreed with Alan Wallace on that. The White House eventually overruled him, and we kept the coffee agreement. When I went to the secretary of state to appeal decisions, such as the threat to the coffee agreement, even if the secretary reluctantly understood that this was necessary, it was always painful for him to overrule his good friend, Alan Wallace, for whom he had immense professional respect and personal affection. After the coffee problem, some people in the White House wanted to send Wallace off to an embassy.

Q: It was a very long time that you were in this amorphous state. Haig was secretary of state for . . .

McCORMACK: I came in October of 1981 and served as a consultant from October of 1981 until Hormats left in 1982. After my dinner with Alan Wallace, he strongly endorsed me to be the assistant secretary. My appointment then was sent forward to the Senate for approval. However, another problem developed. Rick Burt wanted to be the assistant secretary for Europe. He was opposed by a number of the conservative senators because they thought he didn't agree with the president's agenda, based on his writings in *The New York Times*.

Burt was reported to have arranged through his former roommate, who worked for a Democratic senator, to put a hold on my nomination. My nomination couldn't go forward until the other senators agreed to let Rick

Burt be confirmed. There was such antagonism toward Burt in the Senate and the White House that it just gridlocked the process.

In the end, I was unanimously confirmed, as I was for every other position I have ever held that required confirmation. I was simply a victim of a ploy by Rick Burt's friends to get him appointed assistant secretary for Europe, and in the end it worked for him. Prior to confirmation, I was a consultant but was also the acting assistant secretary of state for economics and business. I served as the acting assistant secretary until I was eventually confirmed in March of 1983.

Q: Could you explain the relationship shifts during this time, from 1982 on. I mean, you have assistant secretary for economics attached to your name, then there is an under secretary for economics. Who did what and why?

McCORMACK: The Under Secretary tended to concentrate on a few key issues and on broad supervision. Both of us reported to the Secretary of State.

Q: You both did?

McCORMACK: We both did. We had regular separate meetings with the secretary of state.

Q: Was this how George Shultz ran things? Was this true of bureau affairs and Central American affairs?

McCORMACK: We had a regular staff meeting at the assistant secretary level with George Shultz every morning. Wallace was not present at that meeting. Then he would have a meeting with Wallace and some of the under secretaries. But as you well know, the Assistant Secretary has hundreds of people who report to him. The Under Secretary has a staff of five or six people. One is a big operating job, where you have to keep track of everything from airline negotiations to oil prices to all these other microeconomic problems, while the other tends to concentrate on a few major issues.

Now in the case of Wallace, we worked well together on ninety percent of the issues that we dealt with. I attended his staff meetings from time to time. I would go to his office and we would sit and chew the fat for an hour and a half every few weeks, so he would get some sense of what I was trying to do, what my problems were, and what was happening with the Treasury Department. Then we would have regular meetings with our peers from the Treasury Department: the under secretary and the assistant secretary. The State Department and the Treasury Department totally coordinated every issue. This interdepartmental cooperation was unique in the time I have served in Washington. There was absolutely no space between State and Treasury. We sat together; we planned the issues together; we addressed problems together. They had no secrets from us, and we had no secrets from them.

Q: Who was the Secretary of the Treasury?

McCORMACK: Don Regan was the Treasury Secretary, Beryl Sprinkel was the Under Secretary, and Marc Leland was the Assistant Secretary. We met regularly, the four of us over lunch, to work through our issues.

Q: Of the top bodies, you have State, Defense, and Treasury. You didn't have that relationship, if you want to call it that, between Shultz and Weinberger.

McCORMACK: That involved the Pentagon. There is inherent tension between Defense and State on some issues. They have different portfolios and different perspectives. Both Shultz and Weinberger were strong and able men who viewed things somewhat differently. I had one slice of the Pentagon issue, which was East-West trade. This was at a time when we were trying to squeeze the Soviets in a variety of ways. In this case, we were trying to deprive them of as much high technology as we could. This was a controversial policy. The whole area of tighter export controls was a controversial policy.

When I became the Assistant Secretary, I had a person who was in charge of the East-West trade area who lost my confidence when he strongly supported a computer sale to China, claiming it was associated with weather research. I eventually had my special assistant check this issue out carefully and it turned out that this was the computer that was used in one of the major nuclear arsenals in the United States to develop nuclear warhead design. The building in China where they design nuclear warheads was right next to the building where this computer, the High Share 700, was to be located. It was very clear that this computer was ordered to help the Chinese develop their nuclear warheads. My special assistant, a former sugar broker, was able to dig this information out. When the office director in charge of this issue missed all this, I lost confidence in him and brought in someone from the outside to handle these complex issues. Thereafter we worked more effectively with the Pentagon.

Q: All right, 1982, you are assistant secretary for economics and business affairs. How did you divide business and economics? What is the difference?

McCORMACK: It is a seamless web. You make your business decision within the context of sound economic policies. If you don't have some sense of macroeconomics, you will not be in a position to make intelligent recommendations on some other matters. So economics and business come together. You recall that during the previous Carter administration there was a wheat embargo against the Soviet Union, which caused tremendous devastation in American agriculture.

Q: That was Carter in reaction to the Afghan invasion.

McCORMACK: Yes. We lost markets; other people moved into those markets. It was viewed in the U.S. farm community as a tremendous fiasco and it did cause major damage in the American farm economy. The farm economy had expanded to serve what they thought was going to be permanent markets in the Soviet Union. Many farmers bought large farms and expensive machinery. Suddenly that market was eliminated. Grain prices fell. It caused a crisis in large parts of the farm community. So I made it my business to try to improve the relationship of the State Department with the American agricultural community. They had blamed the State Department for the decision on those earlier actions. So I traveled extensively with Jack Block, the Secretary of Agriculture, around the world to increase the sales of American agricultural products in all kinds of areas.

I also went with the Secretary of Agriculture and the Secretary of Commerce for other reasons. Whenever a secretary travels, he interacts with senior ministers in foreign governments. If I knew the Secretary of Commerce was making a trip to certain places, I would sometimes arrange to go on that trip. Then I would also get in to see key ministers. The Secretary of

Commerce would do his business, and I could do mine on behalf of the State Department or White House. Some of these visits turned out to be of immense importance.

Q: *How so?*

McCORMACK: Well, let me give you an example. You will recall there was a time when we had a foreign policy catastrophe in Iran when Khomeini took power. Our embassy was seized.

Q: *1979 through 1980.*

McCORMACK: Yes, and a very large underground Tudeh Party, the Communist party in Iran, was still lurking. In the intel material was some suggestion that, just as the Soviets had come into Afghanistan to consolidate a friendly Communist government, there was some concern that there were elements of the Tudeh Party that might also be contemplating a coup if conditions ripened. Then the Soviets could potentially come in and consolidate that operation. Iran was an important country, much more so than Afghanistan. The reverses then being suffered by Iran in the war with Iraq potentially increased the regime's vulnerabilities in Tehran. The Russians also had historical territorial ambitions in the upper part of Iran. There was also some concern about that. Thus, when Secretary of Agriculture Jack Block was planning a trip to the Middle East, I arranged to accompany him. We went to see Mubarak in Egypt, Crown Prince Abdullah in Saudi Arabia, and the Prime Minister of Turkey.

Abdullah would later become king when Fahd died. He was the chief operating officer at the time, similar to a prime minister. At each one of these stops I said that I was having concerns about what might happen eventually in Tehran with the Tudeh Party. I mentioned this to Mubarak and Abdullah. When we arrived in Turkey I also raised the Tudeh concern. The prime minister banged his fist on the table and said, "I am picking up exactly the same things. Furthermore, one quarter of the people in Iran are of Turkish origin. We have contacts all through their system. I am hearing this from our people. It is time to do something about this. It is potentially very dangerous."

So I flew back to Washington. About a month after that, there was a huge purge of the Tudeh Party by Khomeini's people. All the top leadership was arrested and we ceased to hear any more about the Tudeh Party.

Q: You kicked off a night of long knives.

McCORMACK: In fact we no longer heard plans by anyone to stage a coup in Tehran. I am sure that the fact that the prime minister of Turkey also had independently confirmed our suspicions was the important factor. They went ahead independently and dealt with the problem. Possibly Khomeini's people themselves picked up some of the Tudeh people, questioned them, and confirmed it themselves. They went after the whole bunch. Who knows what all happened? I moved on to other issues. But you asked why some of these trips were valuable; that was an example.

Another valuable trip that I took was a trip to China with Secretary of Commerce Baldrige. As part of our global strategy to deal with the Soviet Union, we were trying in every way possible way to put pressure on the Soviets to force them to spend. This was, of course, one of the reasons behind the Reagan idea for Star Wars. We knew they were struggling financially. The president felt because we were in a position to spend more, if it got into a spending contest, the U.S. could crack the USSR economy. That was the core strategy of President Reagan.

Q: Was that pronounced at the time, or was it ex post facto?

McCORMACK: It was pronounced at the time. Ambassador Vernon Walters' book and papers confirm that in great detail. Dick Walters was present at early meetings with Reagan when this was discussed. It is a matter of record. There are, of course, those who will deny this happened because they don't really want to recognize the fact that there was some relationship between the Reagan strategy and what happened in the USSR. But the truth is Reagan set out with this strategy in mind. I know that as an absolute fact.

The question was what role China might play in this strategy. When Reagan came into power, he had a very close relationship with the Taiwanese, both for ideological and other reasons. The mainland Chinese were wondering whether the old Nixon policy was dead. However, some of us felt that

China could play a role and that there was some advantage in pursuing the Nixon opening. I certainly felt that way. I went to see former president Nixon, with whom I had a personal relationship from years past, to talk about China strategy. We both believed the U.S. needed to increase export of dual-use technologies to China. This later became U.S. policy. But the policy change required a trip to China. We proposed to sell dual-use technology to China with the exception of three critical mission areas, one of them having to do with the development of nuclear weapons, one associated with sensitive communications technologies, and another with submarines.

Q: How about avionics?

McCORMACK: No, that was not dual-use technology, but highly classified weapons-related technology. The three mission areas were nuclear, intel, and submarine. So, in any case, Baldrige and I went to China to announce this policy. But first I went to Japan alone to tell the Japanese we were considering doing this and to seek their advice, because the final decision had not yet been made by the president. When I told them we were considering this, they thought it was a good idea.

When Baldrige arrived in Japan, I told him we had been given the green light by the Japanese. At this point Baldrige got on the phone and called Bill Clark, the national security advisor, and said the Japanese agreed this should be done. Bill Clark went directly to the president to secure his final agreement. Then Baldrige and I flew on to China. However, there was one thing that I raised with the Chinese. I told them that if they ever used any of this technology to threaten Taiwan, the deal would end.

One evening the Chinese asked to see me alone. They took me to a dinner at a state guest house. Then they said the following: "We are not going to use military means to deal with Taiwan, because we don't have to use military means to accomplish our goal. Our strategy will be to create special economic zones along the coast, little Hong Kongs. Then we are going to encourage the Taiwanese to invest in these economic zones. They will make money and they will invest more. The time will eventually come in 30-40 years when they will need us more than we need them, and we will reel them in like a fish on the end of a string. So don't worry about us using military technology against Taiwan. We are not going to do it because we don't have to do it."

Nearly eighteen years later, we received a private visit in Washington from some Chinese officials. The message in 2000 was that they were not going to use military means to deal with Taiwan. The people pressing that strategy in Beijing had lost power in the Politburo. They were back to the "fish on the string" strategy. Imagine that, those very words, eighteen years later. Of course right now Taiwan investors have over a hundred billion dollars of investments in China, and perhaps twice that much, since most of it came in secretly via Hong Kong or the Cayman Islands.

Q: You were Assistant Secretary from when to when?

McCORMACK: I was acting Assistant Secretary from whenever George Shultz came into office, which I guess was in the summer of 1982, until 1985.

Q: You mentioned earlier that, in the Japanese relationship we had, so many of our people were nurturing that country because we wanted to make sure we weren't ever going to have to fight it again. When you came in, were there any countries or areas where we were saying, "Let's not be too rough on these people, because we have other fish to fry; we want to encourage their development so it is not just Americans selling stuff, but let them have a piece of the action"?

McCORMACK: It is my impression that U.S. trade policy became increasingly concerned about a level playing field as our trade deficit began to mount. Early on, foreign trade was such a small factor in our vast economy that we didn't really care that much. The only thing that slowed further opening of the U.S. market was U.S. protectionist interests. From the economic point of view, and certainly from the State Department point of view, we ourselves gain by having cheap products here to be sold on the American market. The consumer gains by these cheap products. "Trade not aid" was the thesis.

There was also what was called the "positive adjustment program," organized by the OECD. This was basically a strategy of actively encouraging the advanced countries to move out of certain areas to make room for Third World countries to have jobs and to grow their economies. That was something that was never formally presented. The very existence of this positive adjustment program is something I myself learned about quite by accident. But that was in fact the banner under which some people operated. However, as the trade deficit mounted, senior people became increasingly concerned. Thus, increasing pressure was put on the Japanese to restrict their exports, particularly cars, to the U.S.

Many people, though, concluded that we couldn't get the Japanese to open up their market to U.S. exports, and therefore, we needed to slow up their penetration of U.S. markets. Eventually this led to efforts by Treasury Secretary Baker to encourage the Japanese to develop more domestic demand rather than rely so intensely on exports to grow their economy. The Japanese in fact attempted this, but unfortunately they carried it too far as they over expanded their money supply. They developed a huge asset inflation, and they eventually seriously damaged their financial system. To this day, the Japanese blame Jim Baker for that, unfairly, but they in fact do blame him.

After the Plaza Agreements, the Japanese currency strengthened somewhat, the dollar weakened, and our balance of trade stabilized until the 1997 Asian crash. Due largely to Baker's earlier efforts to correct the currency situation during the time when I served as Under Secretary of State, we had the smallest balance of payments deficit in many years.

Some elements of the basic strategy that the Japanese used to penetrate the United States are now being used by China against Japan and the U.S. This involves a variety of state capitalism, deployment of their savings via banks to support targeted sections of the economy, and taking advantage of low wages, cheap capital, others' intellectual property, and an undervalued currency to penetrate markets; while using nontariff barriers to protect vulnerable sectors of the economy.

We have now a $200 billion a year balance of payments problem with China, which is growing every year. The Japanese are simply not able to compete in many areas with the Chinese at this particular point. Some of their industries are slowly hollowing out. This problem has them troubled. They don't know quite what to do about it. They understand the dangers. They are trying to persuade the Chinese to appreciate their currency, just as the Japanese were forced to appreciate their currency earlier. However, the Chinese are resisting. This is going to be an increasingly lively issue and very important for the U.S. and the global trading system that we succeed in this area. It won't be easy or automatic. It will require a conscious and forceful U.S. strategy, now missing.

Q: We are still going back to the '80s. I notice you said when you went to China to set forth your three no's as far as export, that you consulted with the Japanese. Was there a feeling that after the Nixon shokus and all this, that we really need to keep the Japanese informed. Was that part of the Ten Commandments for economic things?

McCORMACK: It was not part of the Ten Commandments; it was my own initiative. Nixon earlier stopped consulting on some sensitive matters with the Japanese after the Okinawa reversion because he felt betrayed by the Japanese Prime Minister on a trade-related quid pro quo that failed to materialize. But I felt that we had a shared interest in consulting with each other on some issues. Also out of courtesy, I felt that we should consult the Japanese since they were the main strategically exposed country in the region and our principal regional ally. Had they expressed major objections to our technology transfer policy to China, and if their objectives were credible to me, I would have certainly passed them on to Washington. This might have influenced what Bill Clark eventually recommended to the President.

The fact of the matter is, when you have allies or you want to keep allies, you consult with them in advance rather than present them with *fait accompli*. So this was, as I say, my own initiative. But I also learned, after the fact, that the Secretary of State had not been consulted on this policy change. This had been a White House initiative, and there had been no meetings held either at the Assistant Secretary level or at the Secretary level on this issue.

I did mention to the Secretary at a morning staff meeting that this was a live issue. The White House, however, did not want to have the policy preemptively destroyed. There was concern that if they had an interagency consultation, the Pentagon or conservatives on the Hill would have made it difficult to execute the policy. The White House wanted to do it for strategic reasons. So this issue was handled by an extremely small group of people, very quietly. This was not a unique situation in the first Reagan administration. When I reported to the Secretary after I returned, he approved of it and said that he had always felt this was a good idea.

Q: What about the White House? This was the time when you had Ollie North and others. I mean later the White House became the NSC, and other parts of the White House became a real problem. One had the feeling that sometimes the President was being treated as almost a figurehead, and there were battles within the White House staff. How did you find that?

McCORMACK: It is important to understand that the President provided the strategic direction. The major policy execution was directed by presidential decision memos. Of course, I was at the State Department. I would be invited to White House meetings. The arrangement in those days was that only political appointees could participate in cabinet council meetings at the White House. That was done so that the President's agenda would be formed and executed. If there were no political appointees available for a meeting, then there was no State Department representation. There was a divergence of view between the Reagan White House and the earlier State Department view from the Cy Vance period on handling East-West issues. That division was mirrored in parts of the career ranks.

Q: You say Cy Vance?

McCORMACK: Former Secretary of State Cyrus Vance under President Carter. As you probably know, there were some people in the State Department from the Vance period who believed that convergence theory was the way to deal with tension with the Soviet Union. Our policies would become more like theirs, their policies would become more like ours, and then we would eventually ride off into the sunset together. This is an oversimplification, but that was basically what was called the convergence theory.

Some of us thought this theory was complete rubbish. That was certainly the White House view. We believed that the only way to deal with the Soviet Union was to go back to the programs we used successfully in the 1950s, which worked to contain Soviet aggression when they were moving aggressively at that time: rebuild the CIA, rebuild USIA, and rebuild the ability to operate with muscle and money in the third world. There would not be cheap Soviet third world victories any more. This policy clash obviously resulted in a lot of broken crockery.

When Al Haig came to the Department, the career people who had been working hard to carry out Secretary Vance's general perspective on the Soviet Union were still in position. During the transition period, some opposed the shifting of policy. There was some White House uncertainty over whether State Department career ranks would in fact support a muscular U.S. strategy or attempt to sabotage it. Everybody knew this was going to be a difficult and risky business. We had lost one country after another to communism during the 1970's: Nicaragua, Cambodia, Laos, South Vietnam, Angola, Ethiopia, and Afghanistan.

The Soviets and their communist allies were on the march in the third world and elsewhere. President Reagan felt that they needed to be contained and driven back. People remembered that Lenin had earlier said the way to undermine the U.S. was to destabilize Mexico and then work with leftist Mexicans to destabilize the U.S. That was Lenin's comments in 1921. There was now concern that Nicaragua would then be used to subvert El Salvador. Then Guatemala would fall and be used to destabilize Mexico. Wars were raging in all three Central American countries, supported by Moscow and Cuba.

Shultz was an outstanding economist and a person of immense integrity and decency. Some in the White House didn't believe that Shultz was as convinced as the President that a muscular approach to all this was the correct path. There was some tension between the Secretary of State and the President at that time, and between the Secretary of State, the Secretary of Defense, and the CIA Director William Casey.

When there is a little tension at the top, it sometimes resonates in exaggerated form down in the lower ranks. I was perceived in the Department, and I was, in fact, a White House person. I had been one of the original authors of the President's strategy to deal with the Soviets' 1970s expansion program in the article that I cited earlier. Obviously since I was one of the policy authors, I was supportive of the strategy. I was also a friend of the National Security Advisor, Bill Clark, as well as the Deputy National Security Advisor, Admiral Nance, the chief economic advisor in the National Security Council, Norman Bailey, and others. I had very little to do with Ollie North. My chief relations were with those three key men and their immediate staffs. But it was a time of turmoil.

Q: How did you find dealing with business in your work?

McCORMACK: I had good relations with the private sector. But I want to go back before you go into this. Bear in mind, when I sat in the Department for all those months as Acting Assistant Secretary, unconfirmed, I knew that anything I did or said could potentially antagonize a key Senator and easily result in my not being confirmed. I concluded, however, that I was simply going to call the issues as I saw them and let the chips fall where they may. I took on some highly controversial issues at the time, and I did what I felt was right. I operated as if I had a full mandate, and in the end I was respected for it. I didn't pull my punches in meetings on anything. After I was named acting Assistant Secretary, I did exactly what I thought was in the best interest of the United States in its broadest context. That is also what I have tried to do in my entire career.

Q: Well back to the business side of things. You are talking about economic interests that have existed since the birth of our country, now very powerful giants, the automobile industry, textiles, cotton, rice, what have you. Did they play much of a role? State Department is somewhat removed from business, and they don't respond well to business claims. How did you find this?

McCORMACK: Dennis Lamb was my deputy for trade. He was a wonderful man who later became Ambassador to the OECD and acting Assistant Secretary. After he later became the acting Assistant Secretary for Economics and Business, he said to me: "There is no place to hide in this job, is there?" I said, "You are absolutely right."

There is in fact no place to hide. You do make many key decisions on microeconomic issues. All you can do is tell people the truth. If you can't support them, tell them that you can't support them and why. If you can support them, tell them that you can support them. My experience has been if you operate in that way, you keep people's respect even if they don't agree with you on every decision. That is the way I did it.

Q: What happens if you are approached by somebody from the very powerful sugar lobby as an example? In the first place, how did you get the information to find out and to fully understand? Did you find the staff helpful?

McCORMACK: The Economics Bureau has a large staff of people who were specialists; some were civil servants and some were Foreign Service people. They gave me their recommendations, and if I had doubts I would get on the telephone and make a few telephone calls. Because I had worked on these issues in Washington and New York for so long, I had a huge network of contacts and friends. So I would consult with people such as Paul Wonnacott, a former senior member of the Federal Reserve staff and a distinguished professor. Hal Malmgren, a former trade negotiator, was another valuable advisor. I would also consult people on the other side of the issue. Then I would make my decisions. Whenever I received someone from the outside who came in to make an appeal, I never received them alone. I always made sure there was another member of my staff there, so that I clearly understood what was being said, to avoid misunderstandings, and to ensure follow-up of any required actions.

Q: We have touched on issues as they came up. Were there any particular issues during this 1982 to 1985 period that we haven't talked about that were major issues to deal with?

McCORMACK: Your day as Assistant Secretary for Economics was programmed every half hour from morning until night. You had to deal with airline negotiations. You had to deal with oil price issues. In fact oil price issues were something I did have to deal with that we haven't talked about here. You recall that when the Iranians had their revolution, the price of oil shot up and it helped cause a major global recession.

In the mid-1970s, we developed a strategy to encourage as much oil production worldwide as we could. The World Bank subsidized exploration and drillings; we did all kinds of other things aimed at stimulating supply. When the Iranian revolution and other inflationary factors came together to force Volcker to tighten monetary policy, it of course produced a deep recession. Over time, the combination of a huge new production base of non-OPEC oil, which we had encouraged, OPEC's own expanded production, and the contracted global economy generated a surplus of oil. The price of oil began to come down dramatically. There was an effort by some oil producers such as Iran to try to stabilize and strengthen the price.

The International Energy Agency was also a source of such ideas, proposing a consumer producer deal stabilizing oil prices at a certain negotiated level. I didn't support that. During our regular meeting with the Treasury Department, Sprinkel, Leland, Wallace, and myself agreed that the market pressures should be allowed to work. We knew the huge global recession caused in part by high oil prices would be eased if oil prices were lowered. We actually sent an emissary to Prime Minister Thatcher, whose energy minister was strongly in favor of cooperating with OPEC's price fixers to try to get as much money as possible for North Sea oil. We persuaded Mrs. Thatcher that England's broader interests lie in restimulating the global economy. Therefore, she vetoed the recommendation of her energy minister and encouraged the price to go down. This, of course, caused a huge turmoil with oil producers all over the world including those in the United States. But remember: unemployment was terrible. We had a huge debt crisis in Latin America, partly caused by excessive recycling of petrodollars made expedient by the higher oil prices. We were also in the middle of a major strategic effort to undermine the Soviets' economy.

This was not a popular decision in the oil industry or even with my Foreign Service staff which was in favor of a consumer producer arrangement to stabilize oil prices. But we did not do that while I was in office, and prices went down. This allowed other parts of the global economy to grow. It served as a huge tax cut to generate purchasing power elsewhere in the economy. I felt that oil people had made a lot of money during the fat years and they could afford to take a hit for a while for the sake of the world economy. Importantly, the Saudi leadership understood that the Soviet economy depended on oil exports, and supported the Washington idea of squeezing them financially. Thus they did not undermine our policy by their oil production decisions during those vital years.

Another tremendously controversial issue was what to do about the Latin American debt crisis. Shortly after Shultz made me acting Assistant Secretary, I was casting for small mouth bass in the Potomac River one Saturday afternoon. A truck drove up to the bank and started honking the horn. I waded back to shore. The truck driver said that they had received a call from the State Department, and that I should call the Secretary immediately. So I went to a nearest pay phone and called the Secretary. He informed me that the Mexican banks were about to close, a potentially catastrophic situation, and that I was to go to the Treasury Department immediately. That was the day the Mexican Finance Minister came to Washington for the famous Mexican weekend, when we worked frantically with him to stabilize the Mexican banking system. But Mexico was just the first in a whole series of countries impacted by high U.S. interest rates and falling commodity prices that caused terrible debt problems and default. The ultimate roots of this mess had to do with the excessive recycling of petrodollars and earlier accommodative monetary policies.

Q: Recycling means that the oil producers couldn't use all the money.

McCORMACK: Countries can always employ cash for needs and investments. During the original oil crisis of 1973-1974, there were three theories on what to do about these ever higher oil prices, which OPEC was imposing on the global economy. One was to allow a major country to go bankrupt, and then as one wag said, "Use the corpse of Italy to flog OPEC into being reasonable on oil prices." The second theory was actually to invade Saudi Arabia. During this time, there were people who were talking and writing about seizing Arab oil. In the end, this latter option was rejected because U.S. leadership felt that the U.S. couldn't just steal other people's oil. The third theory was to recycle petrodollars to countries that needed the money to pay their oil bills and spark economic growth again. The U.S. banks were in fact in favor of this third option.

Walter Wriston of Citibank was one of the principal advocates of the recycling option. I was working at Treasury in 1974 when this was an issue. In any case, the consequence was the U.S. banks in effect became not brokers, but loaners of the petrodollars. The Saudis would deposit the money in Citibank, and Citibank would then loan the money to state owned companies that ostensibly had a sovereign guarantee tenuously linked to it. Much of Latin America in those days favored state capitalism. In Brazil, for example, the government was playing the role that the Japanese government was playing in Asia. So you had Citibank loaning petrodollars to a state owned steel company in Brazil to build and expand. Ostensibly, the loans would be paid back by the profits of the steel plant. This recycling occurred on an enormous scale, year after year.

In 1977, I wrote a speech for the Republican Senate Policy Committee to be used by all Republican senators on the Easter spring break. In that speech,

I said the following: "Banks should be brokers, not loaners of petrodollars, because the day is going to come if this process continues at this rate where there will be defaults. Banks and the American taxpayers are going to wind up holding the bag on this issue." The speech was issued and used by many senators, I later learned. But the recycling policy continued, and the third world debt grew.

When Paul Volker began in 1979 to squeeze the money supply to deal with a huge inflation in the American economy in the latter part of the Carter administration, interest rates rose to twenty percent. Many of the interest rates of Latin American debtor countries were short-term or floating rates. When the interest rates rose in the U.S., they also rose in Latin America. The global economy slowed. Commodity prices collapsed. When it was necessary to roll over loans to new higher rates, the debtors couldn't pay them. All this triggered a third world debt crisis.

To deal with this debt crisis, Under Secretary of Treasury Beryl Sprinkel and others developed a strategy to buy time to spread this problem out over a decade rather than taking the full impact of it immediately. The U.S. government pressed the private banks to keep rolling over the debts. The World Bank and IMF were involved in this problem as was the Inter-American Development Bank. We subsequently worked very hard to persuade our Latin American friends to abandon state capitalism and organize their economies on an entirely different basis, so they could in fact become globally competitive. That meant inefficient state-owned factories would be privatized and transferred to more efficient managers.

Foreign private investment was encouraged, which could bring with it high technology and the opportunity to generate products that could be sold as exports on the global market. A whole series of policies along those lines was encouraged by the U.S. government. They worked. During the time that I served as Assistant Secretary, I would often travel with Beryl Sprinkel, the Under Secretary of the Treasury, to countries of Latin America to encourage them to follow sound economic policies. So Beryl and I traveled throughout Latin America together to meet with presidents and finance ministers, offering advice and assistance.

Q: What was your impression of Mexico and Brazil? Did they understand the problem? Where were they coming from?

McCORMACK: Well, the President of Mexico during the time of the Iranian oil crisis, said, "Our task in the government of Mexico is to distribute abundance." Those were his words, "to distribute abundance." So they wastefully used a lot of the money. Some was stolen. They didn't use as much of it on sound investments as they should have. In the case of Brazil, they built a new state owned industrial complex out of recycled petrodollars, some of which was efficient, some of which was not. After the debt crisis evolved, Brazil signed lots of agreements with the IMF: letters of intent, eleven letters of intent in fact. Brazil didn't fully honor a single one. Brazil's debts were rolled over regardless. In the end, however, we came through this period. We had the Baker plan when Mr. Baker became Secretary of the Treasury. This was superseded by the Brady plan. We wrote off some of the debt. The multilateral lending institutions swallowed part of it, and the rest was turned into long-term Brady bonds, and we moved on.

My colleague in the State Department, Alan Wallace, was opposed to the original U.S. debt management strategy. He basically felt that the banks should be forced to negotiate with the countries through creditor committees to get what they could and write off the rest of it. If some of the banks went bankrupt, that was tough luck on the shareholders. That may be the reason why Secretary Shultz sent me to the original Treasury meeting on Mexico and not Alan Wallace. We decided against the Wallace approach for the following reason. At that time, we were in the midst of the deepest recession since the great depression. We also had high unemployment, and a couple of big U.S. banks did go bankrupt.

Q: Franklin?

McCORMACK: There were major bankruptcies elsewhere, and we feared that a laissez-faire approach to the banking problems risked a collapse of the banking system in the United States and worldwide economic upheaval. So we decided that an interventionist approach was required. It was issues like these, where in theory, you could make a case for letting nature take its course, but the downside risks were such that people were simply not prepared to run them.

Occasionally Alan Wallace and I had policy differences, but whatever disagreements I might have had with Wallace, I never lost my immense personal affection and respect for that man. He was a wonderful gentleman. He also was one of the smartest people I have ever dealt with. Our differences were over practical issues. In a strange way, we complemented each other. It proved to be a useful partnership. What I received from Alan was clearly articulated views by one of our finest economists. What he got from me was to be saved from himself occasionally by making sure that the political and practical side and risks of these issues were clearly understood and articulated before the Secretary of State made a final decision. It did result in tension from time to time.

I have subsequently realized that this kind of tension is built right into the situation where you have an Assistant Secretary and an Under Secretary with overlapping portfolios, both of whom report to the Secretary of State. If you care about the issues, and you are trying to do the right thing for the country, there is going to be honest occasional disagreement between these two people no matter who they are. Emotions will occasionally run high.

Q: Let's talk about trade with the Soviet Union or their satellites. Let's say you want to sell a powerful computer. Some in Congress are all for it; the Pentagon is all against it, and the State Department ends up in the middle trying to figure out what to do. Did you find yourself running into that?

McCORMACK: Yes, occasionally. You just have to try to make the decisions based on the criteria I mentioned before. What is in the broad interest of the United States? Is this, in fact, a piece of technology that is unique and militarily relevant? Is it something that you can buy off the shelf somewhere else? Are you just gratuitously denying an American company the opportunity to export something that can and will be bought from somebody else? Is COCOM still a meaningful operation and if not how can we make it meaningful? We, in fact, strengthened COCOM in the course of the time I was there, and it contributed to the growing strains on the Soviet economy.

Q: Were you there during the Toshiba business, the super quiet submarine propellers sold to Russia?

McCORMACK: Yes. Very often Japanese business interests were trying to make a buck, just like Austrian, Swiss, German, French and everybody else. If they thought they could sneak a piece of valuable technology through the system without getting picked up by the COCOM enforcers, sometimes they would do that. Sometimes one had to deal with violators in a firm way. There was one time before I came into office, during the Carter administration, where one particular company abroad wanted to sell a highly advanced submersible illegally to the Soviet Union. There was difficulty in stopping the sale in time. A covert operation was therefore mounted to puncture and weaken the vehicle on the shipping dock so that when it was eventually delivered and used, it was only used once. That was all Cold War stuff.

Q: How was our relationship with the growing European Community during this time? In many ways, talking about how we developed Japan after the war, the European Community was considered a bright star of our policy. But were we beginning to get worried about this?

McCORMACK: No. We had our innumerable little commercial competitions such as the one between Airbus and Boeing. We didn't like the fact that they were subsidizing Airbus, and they didn't like the fact that our defense contracts, they thought, were subsidizing Boeing. So we hacked away at each other a bit on those issues. The issue that caused the main strain with the Europeans was an issue that I was not involved with: the deployment of nuclear armed missiles, Pershing missiles and things like that, to counter the growing Soviet nuclear buildup aimed at neutralizing Western Europe.

Q: It was the SS-20.

McCORMACK: That's right.

Q: You weren't at that time seeing the growing European Economic Community as an economic competitor, we had better watch out for them, or something like that?

McCORMACK: Hell no! Bear in mind our policy was aimed at generating economic growth worldwide. We wanted to see prosperity worldwide. We didn't like the idea of starving children. We didn't like the idea of countries in such destitution that they were potential victims of communism. At the end of the Second World War, we set out to spread prosperity around the world, and we achieved prosperity around the world. That is our post-war crowning glory, my friend, our crowning glory.

Was I happy that I could see Europe becoming more prosperous? Yes. Did we have trade disputes? Of course we had trade disputes, but in the context of a strong and positive relationship across the Atlantic. One of the reasons why I am so troubled now is that we have serious Mideast-related problems with our European friends. We are going to have to work to rebuild these relationships.

Q: One country that is often not mentioned is India. I mean here is a huge country, huge population, a very large potential market, and it just didn't reach our radar.

McCORMACK: I will tell you why it didn't reach our radar very prominently. India was a country with over a thousand languages and was preoccupied with poverty and Pakistan. We also had a legacy from the past. We had supported Pakistan. India was closer to the Soviet Union.

This was the time of Krishna Menon, and we didn't really have a close and trusting relationship with India. I had almost nothing to do with India although I actually had an interest in the Indian culture because I wrote my dissertation on the Indian communities living in East Africa. From time to time, Indian leaders would come in and see me, but there was astonishingly little interaction between us during the ten years I was in the State Department.

Q: I think it is very interesting because I mean as we look at it, sort of a big economic blank in our . . .

McCORMACK: It was essentially a socialist economy. Its exports were limited. It was a highly protectionist, self-contained economy in many ways. What they tended to export were textiles and low technology goods. The U.S. India Joint Commission was set up to try get some kind of a dialogue going. I don't think I ever went to India once during that period of time. The Indian economy and the U.S. India relationship are now all developing at an explosive pace.

OAS AMBASSADOR

McCORMACK: In 1985 I became the U.S. Ambassador to the Organization of American States.

Q: How did you happen to be made the OAS Ambassador?

McCORMACK: Shortly before the 1984 elections, Joseph Kraft, a well-connected columnist for *The Washington Post*, ran with a column that stated that Secretary Shultz intended to dismiss all of the existing Assistant Secretaries: Chet Crocker in Africa, Rick Burt in Europe, and so on down the list, including me, and that we would be replaced mainly by senior Foreign Service officers. All of us Assistant Secretaries, of course, carried scar tissue from various internal battles during the past several years. However, the White House was distressed at the prospect of losing people they trusted in the middle of a worldwide confrontation with the Soviet Union.

I received a call that day from a senior White House official on an open line, who said that the President was extremely disturbed, and that serious consideration was being given to naming another person to be Secretary of State. He suggested that I take a little vacation to get out of the way while the elephants fought.

Earlier I had heard rumors that my telephone and many others in the Department were being monitored internally. The White House call, which was not made on a secure line may have, thus alerted the 7th floor to an impending potential debacle. Before I could leave that morning for vacation, I received an urgent call to see the Secretary. He suggested that the Kraft article was exaggerated, and that he had in mind a senior ambassadorship for me.

In the weeks that followed, Mrs. Reagan organized a dinner for Secretary Shultz, the President, Paul Laxalt, and several others to come to some understanding about future personnel policy at the State Department. In the end, Secretary Shultz was allowed to keep his position, but was forced to fire his Deputy Ken Dam and others, who were widely disliked and distrusted in the White House. John Whitehead, the distinguished and able former head of Goldman Sachs was brought in as Dam's replacement.

I became the OAS Ambassador. Efforts were also made to encourage Alan Wallace to take an embassy, but he refused to go, and remained in the Department for another four years. It turned out to be a good thing that this transition happened as it did. Shultz subsequently played an important role in the end game of the Cold War, allowing face saving moves by the Soviet leadership as it was crumbling. After several years, I was happy to get out of the line of fire in the Economics Bureau, the strain from which was beginning to cause me some health concerns. Other appointments were made which reassured the President that his interests and policy objectives would be safeguarded.

The covert telephone monitoring system, which apparently was a long-standing practice in the State Department, continued. Eventually, it triggered an invasion of privacy lawsuit by a number of former State Department employees at the beginning of the Clinton administration.

Q: And you were OAS Ambassador from when to when?

McCORMACK: From 1985 to 1989.

Q: What at that time was the position of Ambassador to the Organization of American States?

McCORMACK: The OAS ambassadorship is a job that allows you to have direct contact with all the countries in the Western Hemisphere and to address multilateral issues that are of mutual concern to all members. Of course, the key bilateral policy position in the Latin American region is essentially the Assistant Secretary for Latin American Affairs. The OAS Ambassador is generally an implementer of policy rather than a maker of policy. It is a job, however, that allows you to be a troubleshooter when things go off the rails, which they did in some cases while I was there. It also gives you an opportunity to sit at the policy table and offer your own thoughts and suggestions on what might be done about the problems that exist in the region.

The multilateral problems that existed in the hemisphere had to do with the Latin American debt crisis, the drug issues, and the various trade issues. Of course we also had raging conflicts in Central America.

The OAS job has periods of intense activity and then months of low-level activity. Between the times of tremendous activity, you can find yourself frustrated and underemployed. So early on I had a discussion with the Secretary of State. I asked him for complete access to all of the intelligence information worldwide that was coming into INR [Intelligence and Research Bureau] every day, except for the very restricted material that went to him alone. This was granted. He said, "You will then be able to explain to the Latin Americans what is happening all over the world so they will understand our policies."

A second advantage of the arrangement was that it enabled me to spend time every day with the INR personnel and reports, watching what was happening all over the world, looking at material that most other senior people didn't have the time to review. So I spent an hour or more with INR almost every day when I was in Washington for four years. The first young man from INR that I worked with wondered aloud why I was doing all this. I asked his boss for a replacement, and I got Jim Buchanan, one of the ablest people in the Bureau. Jim discovered that the dialogue that would flow from discussing the material was useful to him and the Department. Once every couple of weeks or so, I would send a classified memorandum up to the Secretary of State, commenting on what I was observing from the classified material. It went out of channels through Charlie Hill. Through these interactions, Secretary Shultz and I drew closer together.

Q: Secretary George Shultz.

McCORMACK: This went on for four years. It also had the tremendous advantage of educating me in the most extraordinarily valuable way about what was happening all over the world. My own intellectual capital increased enormously during those four years. I was the very first one inside the American government who drew the conclusions that there was going to be a huge crash in Japanese financial markets. That was just one of many valuable insights that came from assembling the little bits and pieces of the daily reports into a useful mosaic.

The most important thing that happens at the OAS every year centers around the OAS General Assembly where foreign ministers gather to consider the broad issues facing the region and make decisions. Before I attended my first General Assembly, I asked all the former U.S. OAS Ambassadors to get together with me regularly for lunch to draw on their experiences. This exercise was extremely valuable. I had particularly useful discussions with former OAS Ambassador John Jova. I also asked him to travel with me to Mexico and Central America, where he had also served as ambassador, to introduce me to his friends and to build relationships that would support my work in the OAS. He agreed to do this. So we flew to Mexico, and Ambassador Gavin, who was then Ambassador to Mexico, gave us a very large dinner.

Ambassador Jova was loved in Latin America. He was a man of immense intelligence, absolute integrity, and incredible charm. His wife Polly was just like him. As a consequence of that visit and other things, the Mexican government decided that Mexico and the U.S. would try to work together in the OAS and not fight all the time.

Q: Well traditionally, it has been Mexico versus the U.S. almost.

McCORMACK: Yes, but I learned after the fact that the Mexican Ambassador had been instructed after these visits, never to vote against the United States without prior approval by the government of Mexico. His colleagues later told me that the frustration that this ambassador felt over these instructions was indescribable, although he was a very nice man. I did not know, of course, until much later that this restrictive instruction had been imposed upon him.

I learned in this OAS period that it is absolutely possible to make multilateral diplomacy work. Jova's advice to me was worth its weight in gold. He basically said, "Every country in the OAS has only one vote. The main currency that you have for influencing other countries is personal friendship. So try to take due consideration of the interests of others and be their friend." That is exactly what I did.

Every time I had an opportunity to be helpful to one of my ambassadors or to his country, I took that occasion. Because I previously had the economic portfolio in the Department, I was aware of many issues and had wide contacts. So for example, when Haiti was having difficulty with a pesticide registration problem threatening its mango exports to the United States, I arranged for a year's grace to be given to them so that those exports would not be disrupted while they developed substitute products to spray on their mangoes. Little things like that, which had significant importance for those governments. Also I tried to treat each of these people with the same kind of respect that I myself would have liked if I were representing a small country. I built many personal friendships, which have lasted for years in some cases.

Q: Well did you have problems with the bureaucracy in the State Department, which sometimes tends to treat these governments as being minor impediments to the pursuit of our foreign policy. How did you find dealing with this?

McCORMACK: I did not have an easy working relationship with Elliot Abrams. I bore no ill will toward the man, but he was a very combative and ambitious person. He had many good qualities, and he meant well, but at that time he tended to alienate people with whom he had occasional disagreements. We did not have a warm relationship. That, I am told, is not unusual with regard to the Assistant Secretary and the OAS Ambassador who after all sit in the same corridor in the State Department. He also knew that I had friends and connections all through our decision-making system from my 25 years of past involvement. I had the ability to contact the National Security Advisor and the President's other top advisors, not to mention many senators. Nevertheless, when you got down to the next levels of the system, bureaucracy, per se, doesn't exist. What exists are individuals working in a system. You very quickly find out who you could share ideas with and who you really couldn't.

Secondly, when I was appointed to be the Ambassador to the Organization of American States, I had some Spanish language ability. During college, I had once served as a summer volunteer among Mexican migrant workers in the Southwest, and I had previously studied Spanish for four years. I also knew, however, I didn't have the kind of detailed knowledge of Latin America that I needed. I also knew that because I came from a political background, there were those in the Department who viewed me as an interloper. So I approached Bob Sayre, who had been the career Ambassador to four major Latin American countries and had just retired. He had just led the inspection of my Economics Bureau as his last assignment in the Department. This inspection was totally constructive, and I developed a high respect for the man. So I called him one day and asked if he was really ready to retire. He said, "No, by God, I am not." So I said, "Listen, Bob, why don't you became a consultant to me personally, sit in the office next to me, and you and I will work on this portfolio together." I said, "I am an analyst, and I know there will be times when I will come up with proposals that you will be able to market more successfully with your career colleagues than I will."

By the same token, I said, "I need the detailed knowledge on people and countries that you have as a former ambassador in the region. I think we can make a strong team. Come and serve with me for a year. And then I will do my utmost to have you placed in a senior position in the OAS structure." He agreed, and we spent valuable time together. We not only became colleagues, but also friends. We worked together on many issues. Then one year later I arranged for him to become the Assistant OAS Secretary General for Management. He remained for years in that position and did a wonderful job. I considered this relationship as an ideal partnership in terms of how a political appointee can identify a highly competent person from the career system, work together, and pool the strengths that they each have to advance U.S. interests. Our system operates at its best when this happens.

Q: How about your staff? Who was your DCM and others?

McCORMACK: Bill Price was the DCM, and he later became our Ambassador to Honduras. After retirement, he was named the Washington Director of the Council of the Americas. Initially, Bill felt constricted because Bob Sayre was also there. But he learned to live with this situation, and after Bob went to the OAS, Bill did a very good job as DCM. There were, of course, career people on my staff who had been there for a long time.

I also drew on people such as John Ford, a long-term former career OAS official. I developed a friendship with John Whitehead, the Deputy Secretary of State and the former head of Goldman Sachs, who was deeply into economics. John is a wonderful gentleman, a person of absolute integrity. He served as a kind of unofficial referee between Elliott Abrams and myself to keep the game straight. He made sure that we were constructively engaged. It was important for me was to work well with the new Secretary General of the OAS, whose name was Baena Soares. He was a member of the Brazilian foreign service and was anxious to act as an independent figure, not under the influence of the U.S.

Q: What I would like to do is go around, and hit the major countries and the people they had at the OAS, and how they operated, and how you operated with them. Then we will come to the issues.

McCORMACK: All right. Bear in mind this was fifteen years ago, so I will not have the name of every ambassador at the tip of my tongue.

Q: No, but their approach and how you found them.

McCORMACK: The Organization broke up into blocks. The group of eight comprised the major countries of Latin America. They tended to have closed meetings before the General Assembly to coordinate their positions.

Q: These countries were . . .

McCORMACK: Brazil, Argentina, Mexico, Uruguay, Bolivia, Peru, Venezuela, and Columbia. That was the group of eight. They were the big ones. After coordinating certain issues, they would present us with a unified position. Then there were the Central American countries, and they also tended to operate as a bloc as did the Caribbean countries. I tried to make it my business to visit every country in the OAS every year if I could to see their people and leaders. I spent a lot of time in the Caribbean. Each country, large or small, has one vote, as Jova noted.

Q: Was Canada a member at that time?

McCORMACK: No. I traveled around these countries, getting to know their problems, being their friend, and assisting them in Washington to the degree that I could. Because we had a very popular Caribbean Basin Initiative program underway, we had strong support with the English-speaking

Caribbean countries. I also had personal ties in that region, going back many years, and I used those connections to build bridges to people I didn't know. In Central America, there was a war underway. We often had the support of the Central American countries. At the OAS General Assemblies, the group of eight would try to steamroll the thing and get resolutions passed that we didn't always agree with. I tried to build a competing process so this would not happen. That required considerable effort. John Jova's earlier powerful advice proved to be sound.

There was a case during the 1986 OAS General Assembly in Cartagena, Colombia, where a resolution attacking U.S. economic sanctions against Nicaragua was passed by the General Assembly of the United Nations 94 to 4, and three weeks later it was re-introduced in Cartagena. It was reintroduced by the beautiful and legendary Vice Minister Nora Astorga, who represented the Sandinista government. She was an extremely effective diplomat. That key resolution, however, was defeated 15 to 16. Some of the foreign ministers who voted against the United States in New York voted for us in Colombia. Of course, the results of this vote shocked my colleagues in New York who wondered how this could happen. But it was simply a classical exercise of diplomatic skills where you did some logrolling and a little maneuvering here and there. I was later given the superior honor award for outstanding sustained performance for my OAS service.

You can make multilateral diplomacy succeed if in fact you employ appropriate methodologies and if you avoid embarrassing people. I never held press conferences after successful votes like that. We just quietly pocketed the victory and went on to our other business. You want to make it easy for countries to go along with you. There are people who are involved briefly in high profile public service who want to make a national reputation for themselves and are not above a little demagoguery. This is not the way to get the job done in multilateral diplomacy.

Q: *There is usually someone who has to clean up after them.*

McCORMACK: Then they depart and sometimes cash in on the publicity they have generated for themselves. Because I had intended from the very beginning of my career to be a long-term player in our system, I never had the slightest interest in press attention. I basically wanted to make useful contributions to our foreign policy over a very long period of time. So when you don't give a damn about credit and newspaper publicity, this makes it much easier for you to quietly get important things done.

Q: While you were dealing on issues, did you have any coins to use? I am not talking about money, but logrolling. Can you give some examples?

McCORMACK: Yes, I can. At that time, one of the most influential career diplomats in Barbados was a wonderful man, Peter Lorie. He had made a commitment that he would support the United Nations resolution against us on the Nicaraguan sanctions issue. He was of English extraction. His boss, the foreign minister, was also a very intelligent man, and of African extraction. I noted to his boss that "if we make it impossible to use economic sanctions against the government in Nicaragua, we will never be able to use them against a country such as South Africa, should we want to press them at some point to abandon their apartheid system. Surely you would not want to be party to a process that would restrict the international community's ability to put sanctions on places like that." He promptly reversed the vote. Lorie was so mortified that he got on the next plane and returned to Barbados. When Barbados went for us, the whole rest of the Caribbean joined them, none of whom had much sympathy for communist revolutionaries anyway.

Bolivia and Chile had a territorial dispute, and I began to hint that maybe we would review our long standing neutrality on that issue. This brought the Chileans around. When the Bolivians realized that I was considering tilting on behalf of Chile, they also supported us. So we got two votes on that account. In the case of Haiti, I just mentioned to the foreign minister how pleased I was to help out with their mango exports to the United States, and that as a personal favor, I would be enormously grateful if he could support me on this. He said he would.

The people you sit next to at the General Assemblies are determined by the luck of the draw. At this three-day meeting, I was seated next to Nora Astorga, the Vice Foreign Minister of the Sandinista government. I had known Nora for years before I came into government. I had traveled to Nicaragua and had met her and her Sandinista colleagues. I had talked with her at some length. Frankly, I always liked Nora. However, she was supposedly involved in killing a Somoza general by luring him to her apartment. She was a typical upper middle class radical who was disaffected with the earlier authoritarian political system and went too far. So we sat there chatting amicably for two or three days. It was very clear to all that I was not some U.S. gringo bully, beating up on this little lady. In fact the picture of us in the newspaper in Colombia was subtitled "The friendly enemies." That improved the atmosphere there.

Q: Very definitely rather than sitting there grim faced.

McCORMACK: Nora was shocked at the vote on the sanctions resolution when it came. I had done all of my work quietly. I didn't even talk to my staff about some of my bilateral chats. I quietly circulated and persuaded one colleague then another. When the vote was announced, 16 to 15, she looked at me and said, "My God. This is a strange organization."

When the Sandinistas first took power, I was working with Senator Helms. Some prominent people from his state called to say that the Sandinistas were not as bad as some press accounts suggested. They and their friends were having a meeting in Costa Rica with the Sandinistas, and invited the Senator to join them. The call was diverted to me. So I went to the Senator and said, "These are influential people in your state, Senator, and I believe they are being misled by the communists." I said, "I don't think you should go to Costa Rica and meet with the Sandinista foreign minister and others, but I think I probably should go, just to get a sense of what is going on."

Later, I flew to Nicaragua and met some of the other Sandinista leaders. Several other meetings followed. The message I eventually delivered to them was this: "We didn't particularly like Mr. Tito, former head of Yugoslavia, but we got along reasonably well with him because, while we were not enthusiastic about his economic system, he wasn't bothering his neighbors. If you don't bother your neighbors, we probably won't bother you. But if you start violating human rights and exporting revolution to your neighbors, we will go after you. You need to understand that." Well Borge, Ortega, and Astorga, and all those people assured me that they were not going to export their revolution, and would maintain an acceptable minimum of human rights, etc. Of course they subsequently violated these pledges.

By the most extraordinary coincidence, the day in 1985 when the announcement was made that I was going to be the OAS Ambassador, another friend, the daughter of a former Prime Minister of Honduras, Elizabeth Zuniga, was actually meeting with the Sandinistas when the news came in. She reported to me that the Sandinistas put their hands to their heads and said, "No, no, not McCormack. Now we can never use the OAS."

We were also blessed in Washington by the fact the OAS Sandinista Ambassador, Father Perales, was not a very skillful diplomat. At one time, he decided he would remove the statue of a great historic Nicaraguan hero from the OAS and replace it with one of Sandino, a leader in a 1930's conflict. Every country has its own statue of their hero in the Great Hall of the OAS building. He organized a huge ceremony to which he invited hundreds of press and diplomats to unveil a magnificent new statue of Sandino.

I wrote him a letter saying I would not come to that event because I said, "Mr. Sandino was an authentic patriot. He was also an anti-communist. You basically have stolen the name and the reputation of a decent man and misused it for your communist revolution. I will not be a party to this sham." To my astonishment during the subsequent ceremony, where I was not present, the Nicaraguan Ambassador made his speech, and then he whipped out my letter and said, "Now I want to tell you about the supreme insult that the people of Nicaragua have just received," and he read my entire letter and passed out copies to the press.

This letter, of course, was prominently featured in the press accounts throughout the hemisphere. He was promptly withdrawn as ambassador after he had become the laughing stock of the Washington diplomatic community. The Sandinistas replaced him with an abler man, Mr. Tunnerman, a former Sandinista foreign minister, and the diplomatic struggle continued.

Q: How did you find the staffing of the various embassies of the OAS? Did the people in the Western Hemisphere treat this position seriously or was this a place where you might put someone who might lead a coup against you or somebody's nephew?

McCORMACK: The OAS is more important to the Latin Americans than it is to the U.S. in many ways. Through this organization, they can avoid being faced individually against the powerful U.S. It is their means of confronting the gringos if necessary with a united front. So as a general rule, they send capable people there. Secondly there was absolutely no correlation between the size of the country and the quality of the ambassador. Some of the ablest people in the OAS were from some of the smallest countries. Barbados, for example, always sent able people to the OAS. I had closer relationships with some than with others, but I liked all of those ambassadors and enjoyed their company.

At one point, I arranged for USIA to sponsor a trip around the United States for the OAS ambassadors. So we went to Philadelphia, New Orleans, the Mennonite country in Indiana, the Chicago steel mills, the Boeing aircraft factory in Seattle, and finally to San Francisco. I did that to create a bond with my colleagues. It was a very great success and deepened the friendships between all of us.

Q: Did the ambassadors to the OAS have connections to our Congress? How did they work with the bilateral embassies in Washington?

McCORMACK: They were always a little cautious about treading on the turf of the bilateral embassies. There was no visible tension that I could see. Everybody understood the rules of the game. There is one set of multilateral functions at the OAS and another set of functions that are done by their embassies. I think it was considered a more prestigious appointment to be the bilateral ambassador than to be the OAS ambassador. Sometimes, though, the ambassador would have two hats. Ambassador Tunnerman, for example, was both the ambassador to the OAS and the bilateral ambassador to Washington from Nicaragua.

Q: On the other side of the coin, when you had an issue coming up, how did you work with our embassies to get them to support you?

McCORMACK: The Department sent demarches to other governments, of course, on our views of the issues in the forthcoming OAS General Assembly. The ambassadors would go in and talk to foreign ministers. Sometimes I did this myself. We had wonderful cooperation with the embassies abroad and worked as a team. That is also how our mission to the United Nations works at its best. All these ambassadors are instructed agents. Mostly, however, ambassadors are given a certain amount of flexibility to decide on tactical issues. On high profile issues, though, the foreign ministers decided policy in the capitals. That is why I made it my business to travel to see those foreign ministers regularly.

Dwight Ink, then head of the AID section for Latin America in the State Department also traveled with me from time to time. He would sign large checks for major AID projects, and I would sit beside him at the table while the checks were signed and the flash bulbs of the press recorded the events. Dwight was a personal friend, a man of immense experience and integrity, a former OMB senior official, and a very patriotic and team-oriented man. Dwight Ink's collaboration put the thought in the minds of some that maybe my goodwill or lack thereof might have something to do with aid packages. Sometime it did, in fact. Dwight was happy to support this effort.

Q: There is always a Western Hemisphere person in the National Security Council. This was a National Security Council with a certain amount of turmoil in this period, and we will come to that. But I mean the basic, how did you relate to that?

McCORMACK: I did not have as much regular contact with the National Security Council people when I was the OAS Ambassador as I did when I was the Assistant Secretary for Economics. There were reasons for this. I had a different role, a different mission. There was also a different cast of characters at the National Security Council. I went out of my way to keep a low profile. I realized that there was a certain amount of nervousness in the Department about the fact that I did have easy access to the upper levels of the White House decision-making system. It made some people nervous. So I decided in the interest of good relations with my colleagues and the Secretary of State to minimize that.

I did have a very close friend of 20 years, whom I mentioned in an earlier interview, Bromley K. Smith, the previous long-time Executive Secretary of the National Security Council, who had been kept on as an advisor. I consulted Bromley regularly, but he was not really in the line channel. Bromley was sort of a semi-retired statesman who provided support to any official who wanted to come and consult him. He had a nice office in the EOB. So I did visit him regularly, but that was as much in the nature of personal friendship as it was policy. I never failed to get good advice from Bromley whenever I needed it. Bromley was originally sent over from the State Department by Dean Acheson when the NSC was organized in 1948. A wise man indeed, and a patriot.

Q: Well, Senator Helms during this time was considered a specialist on Latin America. How did that play with you?

McCORMACK: I had a good personal relationship with the Senator from the time that I served on his staff. He and his staff were aware of the tension that existed between the Senator and the Secretary of State, and between the Senator's staff and the Secretary of State's staff on some of these issues. We both went out of our way to avoid my getting in the middle of that. There were some young Hill staffers who threw their weight around a bit and felt very strongly about some issues. I did not engage with them. I had a good relationship with the Senator, which I valued. But as I mentioned previously, in all the years that I served in the Department, Senator Helms only called me twice for favors. The Senator told his staff that I was an honest person who was trying to do what I thought was right for the country. He tried his best to avoid becoming a problem for me within the Department.

Q: There was a woman on his staff who had very strong ties to Central America. Could you talk about her? What was her name?

McCORMACK: I think it was Debra DeMoss. She was hired on the Senator's staff at the time I was leaving. She was a charming and very wealthy young woman from a family that had been close to the Senator for a very long time. She was a likeable person from my point of view. But like all young people from privileged backgrounds with strong views and close to a powerful Senator, she was in a position to push hard for the things that she believed in. The world is a very complicated place. If you don't have the ability to put things in context, sometimes you can see a little slice of reality but not the whole picture. My experience with the Helms's operation taught me the following: Sometimes they were absolutely right, and everybody else was wrong. That must be said. When they were wrong, however, they usually lost the cause.

I have always liked Debra DeMoss. She is now married to a nice gentleman in Honduras. She did not get me engaged in the controversial issues that she was involved in, nor did any of the other staff members, at the direction of the Senator.

The staff member whom I had the closest relationship with was Clint Fuller, the Senator's top aide, an honest person with balanced views on most issues and no personal agenda but to serve his boss well. He was a former award-winning journalist from North Carolina. I liked him immensely. Admiral Nance was also a good and valued friend.

Q: Speaking of countries, how were things going in Chile when you were there? How did they reverberate within the OAS?

McCORMACK: Of course this was towards the end of the Pinochet era. Most Republicans I knew were happy that Salvador Allende had not been successful with his revolution. This was the time, you will recall, when there were Marxist revolutions going on in Argentina, Uruguay, and Brazil. Most of the Republican foreign policy people that I knew preferred someone like Mr. Pinochet to Castro. I don't think they were wrong. However, toward the end of the period when I was in government, Pinochet lost an election and a new government came in. It took advantage of the sound economic philosophy that the Chilean government had adopted with the help of a number of people from the University of Chicago, with an open trading system and a sophisticated macro—economic policy. The only economic mistake they made at one point was pegging their currency to the dollar for much longer than they should have. This damaged their exports. But once they abandoned that mistake, Chile's economy soared.

I tried to suggest to my other colleagues in Latin America to observe the economic results of what was happening in Chile. I said, "Chile proved that Latin America can have economic growth and stability. It is shameful that it takes an authoritarian government to do these things. It is embarrassing to democracy that the rest cannot. More countries needed to learn the good lessons that these economic results demonstrate."

Later, when the Chilean government changed, I said to the new incoming President, "If you come into office and take an economy that was functioning well under Pinochet, and you mess it up, the lesson all over the hemisphere will be that democracy doesn't work. What works is authoritarianism. You have an enormous responsibility on your shoulders to make it a success.

That doesn't mean to say that you need to keep every policy the same as it is now or that there can't be further efforts to deal with some of the poor in your country, but you have to make sure that your macroeconomic policy stays sound and your economy remains open. Otherwise, you will be discrediting not only yourself, but democracy itself."

He absolutely agreed with me. He went ahead and carried out an orderly succession. To this day, Chile is one of the great performers in Latin America.

I basically tried to be protective of Chile during the time when they were under assault from various other places. I was happy to see them moving gradually toward a more democratic system. At a time when we were fighting communism in Central America, I was glad that we didn't have another communist insurgency in the southern cone.

Q: Did Chile have much weight within the OAS?

McCORMACK: Yes, Chile had a very intelligent man in Ambassador Illanes. He was influential because he was able and because he was an exceptionally nice person. He was not at all ostracized. In fact, the OAS non-intervention clause in the charter at the time mandated non-intervention in the internal affairs of other countries. The charter is now changed to support democracy.

In those days, we always spoke on behalf of democracy, but the OAS felt that countries themselves should be able to decide their own governments. You will recall at that time there were also authoritarian governments in Brazil and Argentina after a time of turmoil. This was a time of tremendous transition in the region. By the time I left my job in the OAS, Chile and Nicaragua were the only countries that weren't democracies. Cuba was not active in the OAS.

Q: Jeane Kirkpatrick had sort of gained her political reputation by singling out Latin America and saying we can do business better with these right-wing dictators than we can with leftists.

McCORMACK: I think her view was much more subtle.

Q: Yes, but could you talk about Jeane Kirkpatrick and Latin America during the time you were at the OAS.

McCORMACK: We didn't come together because she had resigned as the United Nations Ambassador in December of 1984, and I became the OAS Ambassador in 1985, so we had no overlap. She was there during the time of the Falklands War when I was working in the Economic and Business Bureau of the State Department. She was in favor of supporting Argentina as opposed to supporting England in that conflict. Of course, Secretary of State Haig was not in sympathy with that point of view since we were dealing with our most important NATO ally.

Q: She wasn't then a presence during the time you were there?

McCORMACK: I never had any direct interaction with her in the time that I was in the government. We both agreed, however, that if you had to choose between a communist totalitarian government and an authoritarian government, it was better to have an authoritarian government. She is, of course, a tremendous supporter of democracy. But anarchy and insurgencies sometimes happen. If you had to choose between an authoritarian system, which is likely ultimately to morph into a democratic system, or a totalitarian communist system like Castro's, which once imbedded stays forever, it was clear to her, and it was clear to me that a friendly authoritarian government was more in the interest of the United States than an unfriendly communist government. The latter government is also likely to be far more ruthless, far more unpleasant, far more likely to spread their toxic virus, and far less likely to create prosperity.

Q: What were the major issues you were dealing with during this 1985 to 1989 period?

McCORMACK: One objective was getting multilateral support for the conflict in Central America so that we were not isolated. A second objective was to secure economic reforms, and in that context I was elected as the Chairman of Economic Operations for the OAS, the only American Ambassador to ever be elected in that capacity. President Reagan sent me a very heartening letter of commendation after that election. We subsequently did a lot of work on economics. In fact we pulled together some thinking for a free trade zone for the region. I was, however, ordered by the Treasury Department to cease and desist. They felt this was not a mandate for the OAS. Two years later after I became Under Secretary of State for Economic Affairs, the Treasury Department, after consulting with President Bush, went ahead and announced the very concept under the title "Enterprise for the Americas."

As I traveled around to different countries, I tried to meet with the finance ministers, economic ministers, as well as foreign ministry types to talk about economic growth and what could be done to improve economic conditions. Earlier I traveled with people like Beryl Sprinkel, who was the Under Secretary of the Treasury and later became Chairman of the Council of Economic Advisors. One time Shultz invited me to join him in a trip all around Latin America to meet with leaders and talk about economic issues.

In early 1986, I wrote a presentation entitled: Obstacles to Investment and Economic Growth in Latin America. It contained all the elements of what was later called "The Washington Consensus." It also touched upon some neuralgic policy issues that were still controversial in the Department. Alan Wallace received a copy of it and gave it to Secretary Shultz. The Secretary loved it and wrote me a letter saying what an effective speech it was. He asked that it get a wide distribution. It was published by the State Department and distributed by the thousands. Every single element of what later became known as "The Washington Consensus," virtually without exception, was covered in that presentation.

Q: While we are at it, what did you see at the time were the major obstacles to encouraging investment?

McCORMACK: The major obstacles were high macroeconomic risks, crime, and a poor investment climate. Sound macroeconomic and tax policies, open trade and investment regimes, plus privatizations were advised. Otherwise investors will invest in other countries where they can make profits. Attracting investment is a very competitive business. I listed what would be required to make Latin America economically competitive.

Q: It is still pertinent?

McCORMACK: It is still very pertinent. It was a generic approach to getting economic growth going again. I have subsequently given it to the Russians after Yeltsin took over. It was translated into Russian by our

Embassy in Moscow and distributed. It has been distributed in French in parts of Francophone Africa. I gave it to President Kufuor of Ghana as he was thinking about running for the presidency of Ghana some years back. He took it and incorporated it into his campaign. Now inflation is way down in Ghana.

Q: Well let's talk about 1985 when you came in. What was the status of Central America and talk about how you viewed it and what you were doing?

McCORMACK: Problems in Central America began when Nicaraguan Sandinistas abused human rights and began killing and jailing people. Ortega and Borge also began looting the country with their colleagues. A disgruntled former Yugoslavian comrade of Tito, Milovan Djilas, wrote a wonderful book called *The New Class*, which described what happens when communist rulers come to power. The big houses of the rich men have new occupants. Mercedes cars are driven by other people: a new class. The Sandinistas became the new class. They started getting kickbacks on every imaginable business angle. That was not the worst part. The worst part was they began serving as a conduit of weapons to the communists, who were fighting in Guatemala, El Salvador, and Honduras. This is what brought the United States down on them hard.

Q: What was driving them? Was it ideology?

McCORMACK: It was ideology. Remember the Brezhnev Doctrine about communism marching in only one direction? Remember the KGB? Remember Che Guevara in Bolivia? This ideology of spreading communism backed by a forceful KGB was a real and a grave threat.

The world was different in those days. Our friends had lost in Southeast Asia and in Afghanistan. We had serious problems in Angola and elsewhere. Things were going badly for us in Ethiopia. KGB supported Eurocommunists were trying to get into power in Spain, Portugal, Italy, and France. At this time, you had this group of Central American communists who thought they were the wave of the future. They were given weapons, money, and assistance by the Soviets, from the KGB, and from Cubans who were the conduits. That was a strategy that went back to the 1920s. So we were anxious not to let that unfold without challenge in our hemisphere.

Of course the CIA was involved in this struggle, and there was some tension in the administration on overall strategy with regard to dealing with communist insurgencies. Central America was part of a larger effort that was being made to confront the Soviets anywhere they were supporting insurgencies, so there would be no more cheap victories for them.

Q: How was this battle fought during your time at the OAS?

McCORMACK: We would have periodic meetings of the OAS General Assembly where specific issues such as the economic sanctions issues against Nicaragua would be raised. Efforts to condemn our economic sanctions on Nicaragua were raised in resolutions every year. I always defeated them. The main battle in Central America was not fought by us in the OAS. The main battle was fought by other parts of the U.S. government. I was not on the Central American Strategy Committee, thank God. Some of the things planned there with Iran-Contra got them in serious legal trouble. I would have been happy to have been on the Committee, but Abrams kept me off.

Q: Well, as we began to build up the contras within Nicaragua, how was that playing within the OAS? What were you getting?

McCORMACK: Well bear in mind that the heavy lifting on that issue was done before I became OAS Ambassador. These were ongoing, up-and-running programs by the time I was there. There was a war going on. The question was, "Was it going to be successful or not?"

There were major propaganda operations underway. The OAS was one of the theaters for various propaganda efforts that were being made to either support or condemn the war. But the real work on the Central American issues was being done by the CIA and NSC. The only time I got involved was when I thought the State Department was about to make a mistake. Then, I would write a memo and send it to the Secretary of State. There were a few times when I did that and in fact prevailed.

Q: What sorts of things were these?

McCORMACK: One of the more contentious solutions to the Nicaragua conflict had to do with commitments of United States and others under the

Rio Pact. Bob Sayre and I saw a few people privately and killed efforts to undermine it. I was also an old friend of Bill Casey, the CIA Director. From time to time, when I wanted to know what was happening, I would go over by myself and see him alone. There was never anyone else present except him and me. If I had something that I felt that I wanted the President to take note of, Bill would do that at his regular morning briefings. I didn't do it very often, only if I felt that something really needed to be brought to the attention of the President for action. When all else failed, this channel never failed.

Q: Did Oliver North ever cross your track?

McCORMACK: Briefly, but only very distantly. I mentioned Bromley Smith earlier. Bromley was the longest serving employee of the National Security Council. He served as Executive Secretary for Johnson and Kennedy and Deputy Executive Secretary for Eisenhower and Truman. Later he was brought back and became sort of a permanent advisor at the National Security Council.

One day I went over to see Bromley Smith during the Tower commission investigation, which was reviewing Iran Contra. Bromley looked strangely pale. I said, "What's wrong, Bromley?" He took the copy of the Tower Commission report, and he threw it across the desk. He said: "Have you seen this?" I said, "No." He said, "This is an advance copy of a report that is going to be issued tomorrow. These people have prostituted an institution to which I have given my entire life."

He was referring to the Iran-Contra people he thought had abused the National Security Council process. "Now this Commission has compromised the whole concept of executive privilege, which I successfully defended for 40 years. I am resigning today." He went home and died three days later. Mac Bundy and I were pallbearers at his funeral at the National Cathedral. Bromley had undergone a medical examination one week before this event, and he had been given a clean bill of health.

Q: What were they trying to do?

McCORMACK: Basically they broached the principal of executive privilege. That was the smaller issue. The main issue was his complete disgust at how people had misused the National Security Council structures. It literally killed him. Anyway he was a great and wonderful patriot. Subsequently, a magnificent tribute appeared in *The Washington Post* by Joe Layton. The headline read: "Bromley Smith, Confidant of Presidents."

I did not have anything to do with any of these Iran Contra events. Later when Bush Sr. became President, I was helped to rise higher in the system.

Q: What about Cuba? Was that much of an issue while you were there?

McCORMACK: No, it was not. We all knew Castro was a gross violator of human rights, and that he was serving as a conduit for guns and terrorism in the region. In fact there were some assassination attempts made against me when I was the OAS Ambassador.

Q: How would that be?

McCORMACK: Well, we had the General Assembly meeting in 1986 in Cartagena, Columbia. It was an extremely high threat environment. Drugs were a very hot issue on the agenda. The Secretary of State came down, spent a few dangerous hours, and then flew back to the United States along with fifty Secret Service men who were there to protect him. They left me with five or six U.S. security personnel. But the killers stayed, and they spent the next five days while I was there, trying to kill me. Fortunately, the Colombian secret service foiled two or three attempts. The failed hit team eventually went back and according to reports machine-gunned a busload of ordinary citizens outside of Bogotá.

A year or so later a powerful bomb was hidden in a street lamp near the airport in La Paz, Bolivia. When our motorcade went by, they detonated it. It hit the car in front of me and blew it halfway across the road. Fortunately, the car in front was an armored limousine. Mrs. Shultz was in the armored limousine. Elliott Abrams, myself, and a couple of other people were in the next car, and it was not armored. Anyone in that car would have been turned into hamburger. We later suspected that they were after us and thought we were riding in the second car, which was where Mrs. Shultz was actually riding. They let the first car go by with Secretary Shultz and went after the second car.

Q: Did George Bush, I am speaking of George Bush senior, the vice president, did he get involved?

McCORMACK: Yes, he did. He was involved in a number of things behind the scenes. We would go occasionally to funerals and inaugurations together, so I got to know him in that process. He had a lot of interest in Latin American policy, and watched it closely. Don Gregg was his foreign policy advisor. Don and I were good friends, so I had a good friend and ally there. From time to time that was important. For example, at one time our relationship with Peru completely fell to pieces. President Alan Garcia, who was from Peru's populist APRA Party, was a very emotional man. Shortly after Garcia's election, he repudiated Peru's debt. He and George Shultz got into a private yelling match at the United Nations on this issue. Of course that was very unusual for Shultz, but it did happen.

Naturally when the top dogs snarled at each other, this encouraged the little dogs in the system on both sides to bark too. The whole relationship imploded. It got to the point where our Ambassador in Lima, David Jordan, was not received except at the lower levels in the foreign ministry. The concern of Shultz was that the repudiation of debt would spread and the whole regional debt management process would become unstable.

To make a long story short, Peru's Ambassador in the OAS, Jorge Regada, was a former journalist. His friends had been tortured before his eyes by an earlier military regime in Peru, but he never allowed himself to become bitter by the dreadful things that he had seen and had been done to him. There was an element of nobility in this man's character that made him unusually influential. And of course he was a long-standing member of the APRA Party and a personal friend of Haya de la Torre, the party's legendary founder. Regada became troubled about the deterioration of the bilateral relationship, and asked, "Would you be willing to go with me to Peru to see if we can put this relationship back together?" So I sent a message to Shultz saying I had been invited to do this, and I recommended that I accept. This idea was opposed by Elliott Abrams, but the Secretary overruled him. I contacted the Secretary's office, and I asked for the Secretary's personal interpreter, Ms. Stephanie van Reigersberg, to be allowed to come with me. Not only was she knowledgeable about Peru, but she was also extremely intelligent and a person of great integrity.

I wanted a credible witness. I didn't have a very good relationship with my colleague Mr. Abrams, and I was concerned that he would be looking for opportunities to sabotage the mission or me. We traveled to Peru, and met with Alan Garcia. After spending hours listening to this man talk, I realized that he was a bit unstable at that time.

Q: Personally unstable?

McCORMACK: He was perhaps a little unstable, but I saw that he had some better qualities also. I told him that I wanted to get to know Peru a little better. So he had his friends from the APRA Party take me around. I made little speeches with my messages, which I knew would be carefully noted in Lima. At the end of the tour, we came back to Lima. Later, Alberto Sanchez, the Vice President of the country, gave a dinner for me as the final event of my visit. All the leadership of the APRA party was at the dinner—35 or 40 people. Sanchez was a very intelligent, 90-year old man, a blind poet. Halfway through the dinner, he suddenly stood up and said: "We have now spent five days with our friend Ambassador McCormack. There are some things that I think are now clear. The United States is not the same United States it was in the 1920s when our party was founded. It is now possible to disagree with the United States on a specific issue without becoming an enemy of the United States. Therefore, we are going to treat the United States as a friend with whom we have a disagreement rather than as an enemy. We are now going to improve our relationship with the United States." All of his colleagues applauded.

I reported this to our ambassador, David Jordan, who was delighted. The next day the Ambassador received a call from the foreign minister inviting him to visit. When I came back to Washington, I found a letter from Jordan. It was just one sentence. "Words cannot describe my gratitude. David Jordan." Peru then began negotiations again with the IMF. They were not easy negotiations, but at least we were talking. In the end, we didn't come to a complete agreement on all of our issues. We did, however, have a cooperative relationship with the Peruvians on most other issues. Vice President Bush sent a note to the Secretary of State saying how pleased he was that we were beginning to make progress in our difficult relationship with Peru. Of course, they sent a copy to me.

Now as it turned out, not everybody was happy about this, but they were basically told to shut up. Later, Shultz ordered that I be awarded the superior honor award for outstanding sustained performance as a consequence of this and other things. John Whitehead, the Deputy Secretary of State, told his staff: "Say what you will about McCormack, he gets the job done."

Q: You fasten on Elliott Abrams as being on a different tack than you. Often subordinates pick this up and start pecking away at what you are trying to do. Were you finding that sort of thing happening?

McCORMACK: One of his deputies was not very helpful, but most of the other people in the Latin American bureau were supportive. The mere fact that Bob Sayre was part of my operation told his former colleagues, who respected him, that we were running a highly professional operation. From time to time, John Whitehead and the Secretary would take a personal interest in our situation. That kept the pressure down.

Q: Well, the truth of the matter was that Elliott Abrams was not the most beloved person within the State Department. He himself didn't have strong depth of support.

McCORMACK: He was his own worst enemy at that time.

Q: Were there any other issues or incidents that you would like to talk about?

McCORMACK: No. We just went on with our agenda. I recruited former Senator Paula Hawkins to serve as my coordinator for the anti-drug program. She did a fine job within the inherent limits for dealing with the drug issue. This is a problem much like a chronic illness, which you can't cure but only manage. It is a problem of demand in the United States and supply in Latin America and elsewhere. There are many complex issues: interdiction, how much pressure you want to put on other governments, the cost, the dubious success of crop substitution programs, the corrupting poison the drug trade inflicts upon governments, the suffering, crime, and violence. We concluded that we were not going to solve the drug problem. We could, however, limit it. The first line of defense was American schools where we had to encourage anti-drug programs. But our approach was inherently unsatisfying because there was no real complete solution as far as I could see. It was just a question of limiting a huge, evil multinational enterprise that was preying on children and destroying both lives and societies.

Q: Was there a view about drug trafficking within the OAS?

McCORMACK: Everybody was opposed to it. I remember Ambassador Lemos from Colombia, who later became the Attorney General. One day he just broke down and wept in front of the other ambassadors at a closed meeting of our council over what was happening in his country. He was a very distinguished man who felt the total frustration of being unable to deal with the problem. I felt tremendous sympathy for this man and the many Columbian people like him. But as you know in Colombia, the drug people offered silver or lead. That was the choice, silver or lead. If you cooperated, you could get money; otherwise you could be given a bullet.

I talked to one Colombian who couldn't be corrupted. Then one day he was sent a picture in the mail of his daughter walking to grade school taken through a telescoped rifle with the cross hairs on her head. He resigned his job and left the country. That was the dilemma of the good people. There were thousands of good people like this. Drug criminals would exterminate whole families. They would even take the goldfish out of the bowl and squash the goldfish after they killed all the members of the family—an odious business.

There is no easy solution. It is one that requires constant effort. Shultz at the end concluded that the only way was to legalize drugs to take the profits out of the business. I never went that far, but I realized there was no easy solution, only a long-term management problem. The menace had to be fought family by family by family.

The human rights issue was another complex challenge. I was able to persuade the former top State Department lawyer, Jack Stevenson, to become the head of the Human Rights Commission in the OAS. He did a wonderful job in lifting up human rights all over the region. It was a pleasure dealing with this able and dedicated gentleman.

During the time that I was serving there, I could see that conditions were improving economically in Latin America, and we were making progress on policy reform.

Q: Also politically too. I mean this is an extremely impressive period. These countries started basically with military governments, and one by one they were moving towards democratically elected governments.

McCORMACK: Yes, absolutely. It was very gratifying to watch that process move forward and to know that you had some small role as part of a much larger effort.

Q: How did the Caribbean islands get along with the different Latin culture?

McCORMACK: Different culture and the historical antagonisms between the English—speaking Caribbean and the Spanish-speaking countries went back to the days of the buccaneers. They inherited some of this tension. One culture was Catholic, the other Protestant. I spent a lot of time visiting leaders in every island in the Caribbean, including Eugenia Charles of Dominica. When these good people needed something from the U.S. Government, they would often come to me. I would then act on their behalf.

I want to emphasize one key point. Shortly after I became OAS Ambassador, I said to my staff, "If we are to be successful in this mission, we need to imagine every day as we walk out of our offices that there is an invisible sign above our door: if we care about them, they will care about us. If we do this and heed our own advice, we will be successful." That remains the heart of any multilateral diplomacy that is going to be effective for the U.S. We were largely successful in our mission because we did care about our colleagues and their countries. If the time comes when we forget this, we will be isolated in this world.

The first thing is to listen carefully to what others have to say to us. You would think this practice would be obvious to everyone, but it isn't. This is a very complicated world. You have to act within the limits of what is possible. If you listen first, others will listen to you. You might also learn something very important.

AMERICAN SHERPA IN A
TIME OF TRANSITION

Q: Okay, well I think this is probably a good place to stop. So in '89 the Reagan administration comes to an end; what happens to you?

McCORMACK: I was invited to be the Under Secretary of State for Economic Affairs by the new President Bush, and I worked with him for the next two years.

Q: Can you describe how you got this job?

McCORMACK: This is probably a good time to talk about how some political appointees get their jobs in our system.

During a campaign for the Presidency every four years, the candidate selects a few key people to help him run his campaign. There is the fund raising operation, the issues development staff, the delegate hunting operations, speechwriters, etc. Primary elections have to be organized state by state. A campaign manager is named to lead the overall effort and help recruit the top staff in the functional and regional areas. Teams of people are recruited or volunteer to write position papers on key issues. These are part of the pool of people who will subsequently be competing for key positions inside the administration, should the campaign be successful.

After the primary elections, the other competing candidates who lost are asked to support the winning candidate. The key staff members of the losing candidates are then explicitly folded into the overall campaign effort of the winner. They add to the pool of future job candidates.

After the general election, various powerful people in the Senate and elsewhere recommend other key people for positions. The President's personal friends also weigh in with lists of people. There are thus dozens of candidates for each potentially available job.

After the election, the transition is formed under a Director. It falls to him to organize a process by which the competing demands of all these potential candidates can be judged.

There are two ways to organize a government: the strong cabinet model and the strong White House model. A strong cabinet model brings powerful former Governors and other political figures into the government and much power is delegated to them. These powerful cabinet members also provide political strength to a President to help him get his programs through Congress, and help him through rough spots that happen in each administration.

A strong White House model deliberately selects politically weak cabinet members to permit the White House staff and their nominees and friends to call most of the shots. Most administrations are hybrids, with some strong cabinet members and some areas where the White House staff has the most clout. The strong cabinet model works best when the President develops close working relations with his cabinet members and uses them as his staff.

The President himself has to make this first major decision. This helps determine how the transition personnel process will unfold. The pattern has been for a President's first administration to be a cabinet-led model, the second term, a White House-led process. But if a President gets in trouble during a White House-led period, he lacks political heavy weights in the administration to provide strength, advice, and political support. Nixon and Bush II are good examples of both patterns.

After the top agency heads are selected, a struggle then begins between the list of candidates advanced by the nominated agency head, and the list of candidates generated by the transition staff, based on campaign service, personal friendship, and other considerations. There is a battle, job by job. Financial contributions become important considerations for some positions. Sometimes cliques working inside presidential transitions struggle to advance their own personal friends and acquaintances. There is usually an effort by some parts of the campaign staff, looking ahead to the transition, to bring their personal friends into the campaign process, at least nominally, so that they can be "credentialed" for subsequent service in the administration. Because of the social and political differences among factions, a kind of civil war sometimes occurs; perhaps it should be called a guerilla war. It is all behind the scenes.

For an outsider to understand what is happening under the transition blanket is left to his imagination. You can hear the shrieks of triumph, the groans of the mortally wounded, and the occasional press leak aimed at lifting up or casting down a job aspirant. To the outside world, this intense, supremely important struggle is largely invisible. Ultimately, the President-elect and his closest advisors choose winners or ratify the selection of survivors of the transition struggle process.

The struggle inside the transition is often more intense, and for the future of the administration, more important than the campaign itself. People are policy.

Sometimes a winning presidential candidate with a long background in politics and government will have his own personal friends and confidants whom he inserts into the system. He then knows what he is getting by way of judgment, perspective, and loyalty. President-elects without a lot of national experience and contacts sometimes have large chunks of their administrations formed by the transition guerilla war results.

Character assassination is often a mere venal sin in the transition job war process. Unless the job candidates have friends inside the system to warn and protect them from the inevitable smears, or a patron so powerful that an appeal to the President-elect can be organized after the preliminary selection process unfolds, prospects for reversing this process for victimized individuals are remote.

During the midpoint of the first Reagan transition, the entire list of politically recommended candidates for sub-cabinet positions was mysteriously erased from the master computer with no backup over a weekend. During the Nixon transition, responses from mass mailings from a Who's Who solicitation so overwhelmed the transition team that eventually it was impossible to sort out the really important letters of recommendation from the tens of thousands of letters of response to the Who's Who mailing. Six months later, the bulk of the Nixon era transition correspondence was, in its tens of thousands, quietly taken down to the basement of the EOB in large cardboard boxes and consigned to the furnace.

The Reagan transition personnel exercise was possibly sabotaged by some insider faction anxious to launch an entirely different list of candidates. George Herbert Walker Bush's transition was also a battleground. Perhaps it would be instructive to describe the process by which I became Under Secretary of State for Economic Affairs.

Having been in the Department of State for nearly seven years, I was ambivalent about serving in another administration, even though I liked George Bush and knew him from our various trips to Latin America. But my staff persuaded me to organize a modest effort to become Under Secretary of State for Economic Affairs. So I contacted a few of my friends in Washington and New York and indicated an interest in that position. They responded with letters of recommendation and phone calls. I began hearing positive sounds that this might in fact happen.

Then one night at about 10:00 pm, I received a call from Don Whitehead, someone I had known slightly from the Ford Administration. He reported to me that he was now working in the transition and had been given the mechanical task of assembling the final book on State Department job candidates that was to go to President-elect Bush the following day. He reported to me that my name and many others had disappeared from the system along with all the supporting letters of recommendation. The job I was hoping to fill was to be given to a man who had actively supported the last two Democratic Presidential candidates, but who was a personal friend of one of the factions inside the Bush transition.

To make a long story short, this situation came to the attention of the President—elect, who directed Jim Baker to interview me for the position. The interview was successful, and I was duly installed as Under Secretary. But for the 10:00 p.m. phone call, however, this would not have happened, and a press conference scheduled for 3:00 the following day would have announced the list of the administration's choices for top State Department positions, minus McCormack and several others.

As it turned out, this event led to an investigation by the President-elect and his staff of what was going on inside the transition process, and the names of the would-be manipulators were duly and unfavorably noted. Bush was an old Washington hand who acted promptly when he first scented a problem. Successful presidential candidates without such experience, however, are potentially vulnerable during transitions by insider factions with agendas of their own.

Q: Under Secretary for Economic Affairs has sort of run through various permutations in the State Department. When you took this over in 1989 until 1991, what was the job like?

McCORMACK: My most important function was to serve as the principal G-7 Economic Summit Coordinator for President Bush. It took an enormous amount of my time and required frequent preparatory meetings with fellow sherpas from other G-7 countries.

The second critical task was to manage an ongoing problem with the Japanese concerning trade inequities: structural problems, de facto protectionism, and a variety of related issues. I helped chair the Structural Impediments Initiative, a major negotiation between the U.S. and Japan dealing with these structural problems.

The third part of the job required dealing with the constant stream of daily and weekly decisions that have to be made by the State Department in the whole area of international economic policy. You are in theory the principal advisor to the Secretary of State on economic issues. But within the Department of State, there are seldom responsibilities for an entire policy area residing with any one individual. They are diffuse so that the Secretary of State has multiple channels from which information flows to him. That is the good part. The bad part is that this causes constant tension between people who have overlapping responsibilities in the economic and political areas where there are often some differences of view.

Having previously served as the Assistant Secretary for Economics and Business where you have hundreds of people working directly for you, I was aware of the potential tensions that exist between the Assistant Secretary and the Under Secretary on some issues. But I also knew how to work the system. A complicating problem arose when the new Secretary of State

James Baker, who came from Treasury, did not know me well. Jim Baker, who remembered the White House feeling that Shultz had been captured by the bureaucracy, brought his core team with him from Treasury, including Bob Zoellick. Bob had a deep interest in economic issues, but he was also interested in every other issue as well, and he was spread very thin. He used to describe himself to the press as "Jim Baker's brain." Baker installed Zoellick as his Executive Secretary and Counselor, two key jobs merged into one person. Scenting a problem, I asked Baker for a clear channel that did not go through anybody else so I would have confidence that what I sent to him got to him. He agreed.

An arrangement was made for me to submit sensitive matters through his personal secretary, Karen, who gave them directly to him. It worked quite well. Zoellick was unhappy about this arrangement, but it lasted. Baker's secretary brought my notes to the Secretary, and Baker would send back a response to me via the same channel. I also had regular meetings every morning with the Secretary along with other people of my rank and the assistant secretary level. The Secretary went around the table to ask what anybody had to bring to his attention. So you had an opportunity every day to interact with the Secretary. But on the more sensitive matters, I learned very quickly, there were limitations to what you wanted to bring up around a table with about 15 or 20 people.

Q: Can we talk about what were some of the things that particularly stick in your mind: the specifics of issues that you felt needed the Secretary's attention. How did this play with Zoellick and others?

McCORMACK: There were many politically sensitive issues that were best raised privately.

Q: What happened on the Japan-related issue?

McCORMACK: We had a much more open market in the U.S. for imports than was the case of Japan. I was in favor of pressing the Japanese harder to open up than some of the other people in our department. My view was widely shared on the Hill. A very strong piece of trade legislation called Super 301 was passed. The second Japan-related problem was of a structural nature. A very strong dollar during the early part of the Reagan period was partly a consequence of very high U.S. interest rates. High rates attracted a lot of foreign money. You had many other countries that wanted to build up their manufacturing bases and were perfectly delighted to see the U.S. dollar remain very strong. That was what the Plaza agreement was meant to address. A strong dollar meant, all other things being equal, that the U.S. manufacturers were going to have difficulty competing. This situation plus import barriers abroad helped cause the Midwest industrial implosion, what was eventually called the rust belt. Unemployment soared in parts of the country during the first Reagan administration.

A basic structural flaw in the overall trading system evolved. As tariffs became less important, competitive currency policies and non-tariff barriers increasingly determined the bilateral terms of trade. The floating exchange rate system was not allowed by mercantilist countries to operate freely. This certainly worsened after the 1997 Asian banking crisis, and the earlier departure of Secretary of the Treasury Bentsen.

But in 1989, I felt that we needed to lean harder on the Japanese to reduce non-tariff barriers and some of the other structural obstacles that were making it very difficult for foreigners to export to Japan. As an example, at one point we pressed the Japanese because we were concerned about Colombia needing something to export besides drugs. So we asked the government of Japan to let the Colombians export their flowers to Japan. After tremendous pressure by the trade office, the Japanese formally opened the market for flowers and removed all tariffs for such flowers. However they also immediately instituted a new customs procedure that required inspection of each individual flower at the airport before it could be marketed. Of course that made the business impractical. The Germans told me that in the case of automobiles, thirty percent of the value of every single German car sold in Japan was related to costs of complying with non-tariff barriers and special standards that the Japanese had established to discourage exporting cars to Japan.

The State Department was naturally interested in preserving a good relationship with the Japanese, and I was also. But I felt we needed to create a more even playing field. This was not always a popular view at the Department's Japan desk, or with Japan's massive Washington based lobby.

Q: *This raises a very important issue—the one between trying to right an injustice, and trade barriers, and good relations. You know, you can have great relations with a country if you do everything they want you to do. But I would think by this point, the late '80s early '90s, that even the Far Eastern Bureau would see Japan for what it was, taking unfair advantage of our open market and their relatively closed market.*

McCORMACK: It wasn't just the State Department that was not totally supportive of being tough on Japanese trade and currency problems. The Japanese admitted to Treasury in 1988 that they were spending nearly a billion dollars a year wiring Washington: providing money to think tanks, former senior U.S. officials, people who had political connections and access to the White House, etc. They created a huge and effective lobbying operation. Thus, you not only had to deal with the political sensitivities that would emerge from the State Department process, but you also had to deal with Japanese lobbying connections to the White House and the press. An enormous effort was made by Japanese officials to shape foreign press coverage of sensitive Japanese economic, trade, and financial issues.

It was widely believed, correctly or not, that if you cooperated with the Japanese during the time that you served in government, and were viewed as their friend, after you left government, you might be retained as one of their lobbyists or industry advisors. One high-ranking White House official was dismissed in part because of improper handling of a Japanese-related matter. Soon afterwards he was given a million-dollar contract by the Japanese to study a possible second canal through Central America. In any case, it was very difficult to keep any secrets from the Japanese because they had so many different opportunities to find out what was going on inside the U.S. policy process.

Q: Was there any effort made by the FBI, the State Department, or somebody else, to identify people who were essentially on the payroll?

McCORMACK: As a matter of fact, after I left government, there was a major review by the FBI of people getting paychecks from the Japanese and other foreign interests but not registering as lobbyists. There was a whole series of proposed indictments that were drawn up by the FBI and sent to the Justice Department, according to media reports in 1992. Many people were taking money but not registering as foreign agents. When the Clinton people came into office, they noted the many prominent people who were involved in this potential problem, including some of their friends, and decided to quash the whole investigation. According to the media, two senior FBI officials resigned as a consequence of this. I have not verified this beyond what was leaked to the press.

Q: What I am talking about, if nothing else, is that you were dealing in an atmosphere in which you felt that you couldn't really trust a lot of people.

McCORMACK: No. I felt I could trust many people. I also felt, however, that there were no secrets as it related to U.S. policy toward Japan on trade issues as I mentioned earlier. When I left government in 1991, I went to the Woodrow Wilson Center for scholars. While I was there I was earning my $40,000 a year stipend and recovering from 10 years in the State Department, ill and bone tired. I soon received a visitor from a prominent Japanese company who said how much they valued my analytical skills, and offered me a large retainer. I told him that I didn't really feel I should do this because I had been dealing with Japanese issues for the U.S. government.

Some political appointees, who plan to be in government for a brief period of time, use government service as a career launching pad for subsequent service of an entirely different kind. These people sometimes leaked. Subsequently, an executive order was passed slowing down the revolving door, prohibiting this kind of thing, and requiring a period of cooling off before you could become involved in lobbying. The issue continues. In one of his final acts when he left office, President Clinton canceled that executive order. This gave his people the opportunity to do things that he had been quite proud to prohibit when he was President.

These are the kinds of little problems that exist in this town. We all know they exist. The point I want to make is that when you are dealing with the Japanese and others on matters of trade policy, there are no secrets. You basically had to operate on the assumption that they knew everything that you were going to do and say. Therefore, when you moved to deal with them from a substantive point of view, you could not use classical diplomatic techniques. You basically had to prepare a power position that you knew was supported by the President and Congress. If you had that power position, you were able to go forward with your negotiation and possibly get some results. If you were operating without this explicit support, issue by issue, you would be politely heard and ignored. That was the complicated reality.

Japan was not the only country where this was a problem, but it was a conspicuous example because in those days they dispensed hundreds of millions of dollars annually wiring Washington, a tiny fraction of their vast trade surplus. Such lobbying was viewed merely as a cost of doing profitable business here.

There used to be a Japanese joke. Where is the most expensive intellectual capital in the world? Answer: Washington, D.C.

Q: What about dealing with the European Union? What were the economic issues and what was your perspective? How about the White House and Baker himself in all this?

McCORMACK: The fundamental problem with the European Union had to do with the very nature of the deal that made the EU possible to begin with. The original basis for establishing the EEC, the European Economic Community, as it was once called, was to give French agriculture preferential treatment within the community and German manufactured goods equal internal access. At the time of the Treaty of Rome in 1958, we were interested in unifying Western Europe to protect the region from internal subversion by large communist political parties; to make them stronger economically, and make it less likely there would be another round of German-French conflicts, which had been so destructive in the previous century. I supported all of those objectives. As time went on, the European Community became wealthier and wealthier.

Enormous agricultural subsidies developed in Europe, which created an increasing distortion to global trade in agriculture. Because they were so advantageous to the French, it was never possible to persuade them to allow major changes. The Japanese also protected their agriculture because the rural voter had three times the weight of the individual urban voter in the Japanese political system. As a result, the LDP protected the farmers through thick and thin. They had all sorts of specious rationale: food security, etc. But they essentially were trying to protect an important constituency in the Liberal Democratic Party. We had great difficulties opening up agriculture trade where we had certain competitive advantages, a problem which continues to this day. The current DOHA trade round is deadlocked because agriculture is not really in play. Years ago, the French persuaded the EU to give them a continuation of the status quo for agriculture until the year 2013. This is going to make it very complicated for global trade negotiations. The developing countries have made it very clear that if agriculture is not opened up, they are not going to open up their other markets to our exports and our services.

During the Bush transition in 2000, I was asked if I wanted to be considered to be the U.S. trade negotiator. No doubt I was one of many who were asked this question by the White House during the transition. I said no. I could see there was no consensus internationally or domestically for moving forward with the ambitious Bush trade agenda that had emerged during the campaign. Thus, I suspected that whoever got the trade job would find it very difficult to achieve progress on the bigger issues. My former colleague, Bob Zoellick, later found it a daunting assignment indeed. I never regretted my decision.

Obviously the EEC was an important element of our Cold War strategy. There were important communist parties in France and Italy and smaller ones in Spain and Portugal. It was very important for us to make sure that Europe hung together as part of a bloc to keep the Soviets out of Western Europe, and not allow subversion of democratic governments by these communist parties, which were supported financially and politically by the USSR and satellite countries. Strengthening the European Community was one of our ways of advancing this objective. It was very successful. It was successful from an economic, military, and social point of view. The EEC was one of the many triumphs of the post-war period for which our predecessors deserve immense credit. We ourselves executed the containment strategy that they conceived, made some needed modifications, and brought the cold war to a happy conclusion. Eisenhower had foreseen this when he predicted that the Soviet Union would decay from within because of its own internal contradictions. We helped expedite that process by putting economic and political strain on it.

Q: Well, now, how did you view our foreign policy within the United States?

McCORMACK: In what sense?

Q: I mean were we as open or protective as say the Europeans or the Japanese?

McCORMACK: We have our indirect trade subsidies on agriculture, which are in fact less than one quarter of the subsidies of the European Community. There were times when the Europeans would use direct export subsidies to facilitate their exports. I felt countering them was sound U.S. policy, hoping in the end, as George Shultz hoped, that when it became clear to them that we were going to do the same thing, that we could eliminate the export subsidies. To some degree, that happened. Trade policy is kind of an interesting deal. It is very public. Powerful political interests are involved on both sides. Elections in democracies are involved and large numbers of people have their jobs at stake. It is a situation where you can't just operate secretly, particularly as trade has a larger and larger impact on your overall economy.

It becomes a very public and very political issue. That is why enormous political skills are necessary to manage the process. You have to take the political considerations into account when you are considering what you are going to do. If you don't, and you get a powerful Senator who blocks your proposal because it impacts negatively on important parts of his constituency, you have not done anybody a favor by putting yourself into that situation. So there is a constant behind the scenes negotiation process between the affected constituencies, between the powerful Senators and Congressmen who are involved.

Worse, if you, as a policy advisor, get your presidential candidate in the crosshairs of a potentially deadly trade policy issue, you have jeopardized everything else that this candidate might have accomplished as President.

We basically need to develop a new consensus about what trade initiatives make sense for the country. You have to appeal to people to look for the broader national interest. Our broader national interest has changed somewhat since the end of the Cold War, and particularly since the accumulation of enormous trade deficits and net debt that we now have to service. Our currency is weakening because of this trade deficit. In the end of the day we are going to have to export more and import less to service this trade deficit because you ultimately have to pay for what you import by selling exports and assets, or accumulating more long-term debt by borrowing from trade surplus countries like Japan and China.

Q: It hadn't happened yet, but was there talk about the euro, and how did you view this common currency? What was the feeling at the time?

McCORMACK: I was ambivalent about it. The political considerations dominated. During the time I served as Under Secretary, this debate was internal. We basically told the Europeans that this was their decision. This is not one where the U.S. put its thumb on the scales because you could see where there were going to be potential adjustment problems. You had an economy like Germany's that was rich, powerful, and competitive, with a very strong currency, diluted with Greece, Portugal, Italy, and others with less of a tradition of macroeconomic stringency and the other things that made the German economy so successful. We felt there were possibly going to be long-term problems with the euro. As a matter of fact, one of my friends at the German Central Bank told me that a number of major German economists had met with Chancellor Kohl to protest the idea of ending the D-mark and merging with these other currencies to form the euro. Kohl basically said to them, "Gentlemen you are economists. This is a political decision, and you are incompetent to make a judgment on politics."

The whole generation of Germans who lived through the horrors of the Second World War wanted no more wars. They had seen their homes and cities ruined and their family members killed. Kohl wanted to link Germany so tightly to Europe that it could never again contribute to the kind of wars that occurred three times in the previous century. He felt a common currency would support this objective.

The British declined to participate. They knew that to have one monetary policy for a continent as diverse as Europe is an extremely difficult thing to manage long term in the absence of very flexible labor markets and fiscal discipline. For example, one might have a relatively high inflation in Holland, 3 or 3 ½ %. But with one monetary policy for the whole currency zone, your flexibility is limited. If you are not able to use monetary policy selectively to deal with slumps and inflation, then you have to use fiscal policy. That is a much more complicated thing to do, partly because Maastricht criteria limit what you can do in fiscal policy. So it effectively puts all of Europe into a kind of monetary and economic straitjacket unless the Maastricht criteria are abandoned, which will soon create other serious problems, including bond market difficulties.

One monetary policy works for the United States because we have a tremendously mobile labor force. People in the U.S. go where the jobs are. But when you have linguistic and cultural differences as you do all over Europe, you do not have the ability to pick up your family and move easily from Athens to Oslo to get another job. You are still a cultural foreigner regardless of the law. So there is much less mobility in Europe except with the super elite and certain laborers. The euro will trigger continual political and adjustment problems. European leaders have taken this all upon themselves. This is their project; this is their thing. Italy and Greece are two weak links in the chain. There are others. We wish them well. It seems likely to me that the euro will ultimately succeed. We have to understand, however, that it is going to be a bumpy road from time to time.

Q: I was wondering if we were looking down the pike a bit at Europe; particularly France and Germany; and also Japan and looking at demographics. They are getting older, and they have these very expensive social programs. The French are now trying to do something about it. Were we looking at this from a demographic point of view and seeing this as a weakness in their situation and maybe not so bad for us?

McCORMACK: If we were in the 19th century, this consideration would be very powerful and compelling, because in the 19th century the economy was based upon a very large labor force, toiling in highly labor intensive activities. All production had a very high labor component associated with it. Today in the increasingly mechanized world, labor becomes a smaller and smaller component of overall production. You need fewer people working shorter hours to produce ever larger quantities, everything from food to computer chips. There is no apparent reason why Europe cannot effectively support itself and its older citizens, if they make the adjustments that are necessary and keep increasing productivity.

If you have a welfare fund with more going out than coming in, you have to either get more taxes or provide weaker benefits. Sooner or later the need for this becomes obvious to everybody. It will also become obvious to us in the United States. Then a commission such as the earlier Social Security Commission will recommend changes. Legislatures will debate and ultimately act. The same thing will happen in Europe, without a doubt. Will it happen as soon as we'd like? No, but it will ultimately happen, in my view, because it is necessary.

Q: From your perspective at the time you were in the State Department, you were looking at this and did not see this as a particular weakness or problem.

McCORMACK: We knew that it was a long-term problem. One also assumed that sooner or later when you have a vast program that is not actuarially sound this will become obvious to enough people. Politics will then do its thing; democracy will do its thing; speeches will be made; commissions will be established; changes will be made. Bear in mind a political appointee, who is in an office for a brief period of time, manages this policy debate for a short time. You start by building public awareness. You conceive strategies. To make these strategies work, you have to build a consensus. For major issues, this process can take years.

In the case of Japan, I decided after I left government to continue to provide my analytical services free to my successors and give them the benefit of everything that I had learned in dealing with Japan. Every year I do a major review of global economic trends, including the Japanese financial system. These reports were read by top people in successive administrations, beginning with Lloyd Bentsen when he was Secretary of the Treasury.

In 1997, the White House asked me if I wanted to be considered for Ambassador to Japan. So I know this work had some value. Each of us has some area of expertise. People who have done the Arab-Israeli issue very often offer their advice and thoughts to successive administrations as they move on. The period where you actually have power is brief. Power in our system consists mainly of sitting around a table, making your points known to your colleagues, and trying to persuade them. The second bit of power that you have is the ability to hire people and therefore magnify the point of view that you would like to see expressed within the system. But it is a very diluted thing because so many people have overlapping portfolios. There are always at least three different agencies that are watching the same issue that you are watching not to mention your other colleagues in your own agency. You have to be able to justify what you are doing and sell what you are proposing.

Q: You mentioned that a major part of your business was preparing and executing an Economic Summit. What was that?

McCORMACK: Two Economic Summits, 1989 and 1990. In the 1970s to cope with the great economic turmoil that the OPEC oil price increases caused, a series of Economic Summits involving the heads of government were organized. First, five countries were involved; now it is the Group of Eight. While I was there, seven were involved. The process culminated in a summit once a year at the level of Presidents and Prime Ministers to consider the key economic issues facing the world. During the mid-1970s, a serious mistake was made at a poorly staffed Economic Summit in which all the members committed to reflate simultaneously. It helped trigger a global inflation and other disasters. The correction under Paul Volcker resulted in a major global recession complicated by a second oil price increase. But experts learned the danger of poorly staffed Economic Summits and moved to increase the technical preparations. This avoided well-intentioned heads of government being steamrolled into making ill-advised commitments on technical economic issues that they didn't fully understand.

The second lesson learned at past Economic Summits was that if the preparatory staff did not resolve major issues privately in their meetings, it sometimes resulted in big problems. After the Economic Summit involving Reagan and Mitterrand in Paris in 1982, Reagan and Mitterrand issued conflicting statements as to what the G-7 had decided on East-West trade, and what was intended on major global strategy toward the Soviet Union. Reagan felt betrayed, and Mitterrand felt angry. It so soured their relationship that shortly after this meeting, a secret White House emissary went to France and basically said that if the French didn't become more supportive in containing the Soviet Union's recent pressure abroad, all of the nuclear cooperation agreements with the French would be abrogated. This never reached the newspapers.

The point I want to make is that a badly staffed summit helped cause a degree of permanent estrangement between Mitterrand and Reagan. Years later the relationship was still so strained that during a G-7 Summit in Ottawa when President Reagan was walking down a path, Mitterrand saw him coming and hid behind a tree so he wouldn't have to shake his hand. This was witnessed by the Secret Service. Now obviously Reagan was free market-oriented, and Mitterrand in the early period of his career was a socialist. That subsequently was modified. But during that period, they were both feeling their oats from an ideological point of view. That early bumpy summit was not a happy event. The U.S. sherpa at the time, Bob Hormats, was subsequently asked to leave government.

Q: You might explain what a sherpa is.

McCORMACK: The sherpa is the principal official responsible for organizing the preparatory work for the global Economic Summits. Each President and Prime Minister appoints one such individual to represent himself.

Q: You might just explain the origin of the sherpa.

McCORMACK: The sherpa, of course, was originally an individual supporting a man trying to climb Mt. Everest. Basically the economic sherpa is supposed to make sure that the summit is a successful one for the leader. Before Bob Hormats left, there were a few nasty articles in the newspapers saying he hadn't done this and that. Some of it was very unfair. I became his successor as Assistant Secretary of State.

In any case, the first lesson of Economic Summits is to make sure that they are well prepared so that the leaders don't make mistakes based on lack of information. The second is to try to prevent explosive blow-ups between the leaders at the table, which can then poison their subsequent relationships. That means any yelling and screaming that is done over important clashing economic interests is done in the secret meetings that Sherpas have with their colleagues. Many of the key issues of international economics are discussed in private in such meetings. Deals are made. Understandings are reached. Problems are thrashed out, and everybody has an absolutely clear idea of what each government will stand for at that time. Before sherpa meetings, sherpas have detailed preparatory sessions involving dozens of experts from within each government. Thus, once you went to that meeting, you were extremely well-briefed on every single issue.

The Economic Summit communiqués were prepared in draft well in advance. Those communiqués are very long documents, and they covered the whole breadth and range of international economic issues being considered. The draft communiqué basically serves as an internal discussion document. You start with the first paragraph dealing with the macroeconomic issues. Then you move to trade issues, China's involvement with the World Bank after Tiananmen Square, global warming and the ozone layer problems. It also included discussions on immigration policy and so on.

This first draft is prepared by the host country. Some people watching these summits who don't understand what is happening may say this communiqué is so much bullshit because it was prepared in advance. Some say the heads of governments are performing in a sort of orchestrated kabuki. What they don't understand is that sherpas are instructed agents representing their governments and leaders. You can suggest policies, but you have to reflect your leader's actual views. The U.S. sherpa is representing the President of the United States and his government. When you take a position on an issue, it is the position of the U.S. government.

The second part of the actual Economic Summits is very different. These involve lunches and dinners where the Heads of State get into the issues that have not been solved by the Sherpas, and where they discuss very topical issues that have just happened in the last three or four weeks such as Tiananmen Square or Eastern Europe's evolution. These Economic Summits are where leaders have opportunities to interact with each other and build deeper friendships and relationships. It makes them feel more comfortable on an individual basis to pick up the telephone later and call each other when they have a subsequent problem or a question. A lot of preparatory work is necessary to prepare a President before he attends a summit. He has to understand what the neuralgic issues are. From time to time, a President can get ambushed in an Economic Summit. I will give you an example of what nearly happened to Bush in the Houston Economic Summit on one particular key issue.

Q: Which year was that?

McCORMACK: 1990. At the Houston Economic Summit, one of the key issues was whether agriculture should be involved in the Uruguay Round trade negotiations and to what extent. The Europeans were naturally anxious to minimize that because of French objections and other European interests. So the European leaders, who always meet together before an Economic Summit, had planned their strategy well. They had given Mrs. Thatcher, who had the closest personal relationship with President Bush, the task of carrying the agricultural issue for them, in return for something else that the British wanted. In these actual summit meetings, you sit alone in the room behind the President. You are the only other U.S. person in that room. From my chair, I could see that Mrs. Thatcher was skillfully undermining the U.S. position on agriculture in the Uruguay Round and moving to try to get a commitment from the President. It was very technical, and he didn't totally understand what was happening. Nor should he have. The President is a man with broad global responsibilities. You wouldn't expect him to be an expert on every chapter of the Uruguay Round brief. So I went up and whispered into his ear that maybe we should have a short recess.

After the recess, the meeting resumed and President Bush backed off from what Mrs. Thatcher was pressing him on. We moved on. To send an unstaffed, new American President into an Economic Summit meeting with other leaders who have been involved in these issues for years is risky. Commitments could be made which are disadvantageous to U.S. economic interests. For years some Europeans have tried to eliminate the staffing from the Economic Summits, or dramatically reduce the staffing of the Economic Summit process, precisely so they could get an inexperienced President to make commitments that would subsequently limit the ability of U.S. negotiators to advance the U.S. agenda. Every sherpa subsequently has warned his successors not to let this happen. I certainly did when the Clinton people came in.

Q: This gives a real insight. While you were there, two major things happened. One was the collapse of the Soviet Empire, and the other was Tiananmen Square. These must have had a profound economic consequence.

McCORMACK: They did, and we have to discuss them separately. In the case of the collapse of the Soviet Union, this was a slow motion process. It still took many people by surprise. One legacy of the Reagan administration was building up the economic pressures and engaging the Soviets in an arms race that strained their economic system to the point where it basically fell apart. Providing stingers and other things to the Afghan rebels demoralized the Russian army, as happened to us in Vietnam. When President Bush came into office, the other boxer was on the ropes and staggering. Dick Walters made a speech early in 1989.

Q: This was Vernon Walters?

McCORMACK: Yes, Vernon Walters was our Ambassador in Germany then. He made a speech saying that the Wall was going to come down in a matter of months. One of my colleagues at the State Department made very denigrating remarks about Dick Walters at the Secretary's staff meeting after Walters' prediction. Walters was proven to have been correct. Walters was a friend, who subsequently reported all this background to me in some detail. His long-standing connection with the intelligence services allowed him to see things that very few other people understood. He had insights from East German churches and evidence of demoralization of the party within East Germany. He could see East Germany coming apart at an incredible pace.

Just before the Economic Summit in Paris in July 1989, President Bush flew to Eastern Europe, met with Polish leaders and others to personally assess what was really going on. His assessment formed a major part of the discussion that occurred in private between the Heads of Government at the Summit in Paris. In the meantime, the President had moved forward with the last phase of the Latin American debt crisis strategy—the Brady plan. He also launched many other initiatives. Virtually all the President's objectives were reached at the Summit in 1989.

Jacques Attali, the French sherpa, was a difficult and complicated man. Mitterrand once joked to Bush that Attali was his idea man, and that he had a new idea every day. Mitterrand said, however, that he only accepted one Attali idea per month. True to form in this summit, Attali came up with some unworkable ideas in addition to some good ones. He had a fixation to launch a massive flood control project for the river in Bangladesh, which periodically flooded. I eventually had to send for the U.S. Corps of Engineers to survey the river and make it obvious to everybody why no flood control project could deal with it given its hydrology and its enormous volumes of water. The whole country of Bangladesh was a flood plain. But it was very difficult to get Attali off of that idea. He also wanted to solve third world debt by printing a huge amount of SDRs at the IMF.

Q: What are these?

McCORMACK: Special Drawing Rights, sometimes called paper gold, but basically money printed by the IMF. He pressed on and on. At one point, he suspended the meeting. He said he had a surprise for us. So he took us down into the basement of Rambouillet Castle where troops were drawn up in formation and presented us with the Legion d'Honneur. Sir Nigel Wick, the able British sherpa, refused it because he said he could not accept a foreign decoration without prior agreement by his government.

All the rest of us became members of the Legion d'Honneur. Then we went back up to the meeting room. Later Attali said, "Now we are again going to discuss the issue of the Special Drawing Rights." I replied, "We already had a plan for dealing with the third world debt issue. It is called the Brady Plan. I could not accept this Special Drawing Rights proposal, which would be inflationary, without explicit orders from the U.S. Government which would not be forthcoming." Whereupon he leaped to his feet and screamed at me, "I will never forgive this, and I will never forget this." I said, "Jacques, let's move on to the next issue." Anyway, you get the point.

Q: Were there divisions in the sherpa group? You did two meetings, didn't you?

McCORMACK: There were a half dozen such preparatory sessions for both of the economic summits, which I helped organize.

Q: I mean did you find that the sherpas tended to gather into factions or not?

McCORMACK: Yes. It was largely a group of six to one. I had the support of Hans Tietmeyer, Wicks, the Canadians, and most others. Obviously most also thought the U.S. should do more things to correct our fiscal macro policy than we were able to do at the time. The point I want to make is there was a lot of congeniality among the sherpas. Subsherpas supported us and were themselves high-level people from the ministries. The key French subsherpa, Jean-Claude Trichet, is now the Head of the European Central Bank. The German sherpa, Hans Tietmeyer, became head of the Bundesbank. The Japanese sherpa, Mr. Kunihiro, also rose to higher glory in his system. You all bond in a way. Many of us are still in touch after these many years. It is an informal global network of mutual trust.

Q: I want to return to what was happening in Eastern Europe and the Soviet Union during this time. Were you keeping an eye out on this as being a major development?

McCORMACK: Of course we were. We wanted this process to evolve peacefully. We didn't want another 1956 process with the Red Army streaming across the border and a blood bath. This did not happen for a variety of reasons. The most important one was that Gorbachev himself was not a bloody-minded man, and Gorbachev's wife was a moderating influence. In Russia, Jakob Yakovlev was a very important advisor to Gorbachev, a member of the Politburo. He was also not a bloody-minded man. Shevardnadze, the Foreign Minister of Russia, was valuable in the process. Finally, the generals had been so chastened and demoralized by the failure in Afghanistan, that when things began to come apart in Eastern Europe, the rest of the system was not prepared to support the Brezhnev Doctrine by ordering the Red Army to recapture Eastern Europe. Of course by then, the economic situation in the Soviet Union was catastrophic, and there were economic reasons why it would have been very difficult for the Soviets to have supported major military operations. For a variety of economic and political reasons, a peaceful revolution in Eastern Europe was allowed to go forward.

The second important dimension was that President Bush made it quite clear to Gorbachev that he would not take strategic advantage of that situation. There were some understandings given that we would not move into the vacuum militarily. Some Russians to this day feel that we betrayed them by expanding NATO to Eastern Europe. This caused some tension and is one of the issues that arose during the debate over the expansion of NATO. President Bush persuaded Gorbachev that he would not take strategic advantage of this situation. Gorbachev trusted Bush. If President Bush gave you his word, you had a deal. We did try to consolidate freedom in Eastern Europe. In sherpa meetings, we discussed the idea of a European Bank for economic development in Eastern Europe. This was originally a French proposal. They wanted to take the organizational structure of the World Bank, duplicate it in Europe, and have Europeans effectively run and use this as a vehicle to develop Eastern Europe's economy and provide money for ecological and other projects.

Jacques Attali was very anxious to become the President of this bank. I did not think he would make a good President for the European Bank for Economic Development, and I did my best to stop it. I went, in fact, to see a senior advisor to Kohl, to appeal to him not to let this happen. By then, Mitterrand had called Kohl and made a deal, which involved Attali getting this job. In the U.S., Secretary Baker, who had a very low regard for Attali from previous dealings with the man, went to the Treasury and tried to persuade Brady to oppose it. But in the meantime, Treasury staff had obviously made some kind of deal with the French and had persuaded Brady to go along with it. Baker said at the meeting, "if Jacques Attali is the President of this bank, we should not have anything to do with it, because it will be a disaster." Brady didn't pay any attention to him. Jim Baker got up from his chair, sat down alone at the end of the table, and read the newspaper for the rest of the meeting as a complete gesture of contempt.

We eventually did set up the EBRD. I felt we should be involved and remain linked to the institutions of Europe. It was one more bridge that would link Europe to the United States. Since we were the biggest player, we felt we should also be the senior stockholder in the exercise. That deal was eventually closed. Subsequently, Attali became President of this bank and confirmed Baker's prediction. He spent huge amounts of money for the most expensive marble that could be imported from Italy. He imported chefs from France to provide gourmet meals for himself and his friends. The bank eventually became so mismanaged that Attali became a public embarrassment to his government. He was withdrawn after banner headlines in the *Financial Times* screamed for his scalp. Attali was replaced by a very competent French official, who had previously directed the IMF. He created order out of the chaos, and the EBRD has subsequently gone on to do useful work.

The second Summit I supported for President Bush was in Houston in 1990. It was a big deal for the President politically, as he comes from Texas, and the Houston establishment had played an important role in his political career. His Houston friends wanted the G-7 Summit in their city. The President concurred. Houston was a good choice, and the people of Houston did everything they could to be hospitable. The Economic Summit took place, and it was a success. However, President Bush's Economic Summit was marred by the fact that one of his sons was unfairly snared in a savings and loan scandal at the time. Bush knew his son was a person of integrity, and was being dragged through the dirt for political reasons. The story broke on the very weekend of the Economic Summit. Bush was embarrassed. More importantly, he felt pain for his son.

You could also see at the meetings between the President and the other heads of government, how much his peers liked and respected George Bush.

Bush was an extremely likable and decent man of great experience who had a very broad vision for the world. He was worthy of their respect.

Q: You know, looking at it from a professional point of view, he was a superb diplomat.

McCORMACK: He **is** a superb diplomat.

Q: And he was able to call people and . . .

McCORMACK: As a matter of fact, in the preparatory meetings in the Oval Office, which I had with him, Baker would sometimes come with me. When we would arrive, the President would talk before getting into our issues. The President would say I was just talking to the Prime Minister of X, and he feels such and such. They would discuss it back and forth, and the Secretary would go back to the Department and implement what the President wanted done. There was never as deep a public understanding as there should have been of the strategic direction that President Bush was personally providing his administration in the foreign affairs area. In his Secretary of State, he had an incredibly effective and loyal dealmaker and tactician who steadily grew in his job. They made a tremendous team.

Q: The more one looks at it, everything happened so fast. I think historians sometimes forget how the collapse of the Soviet Empire, and I use that term, came about with Germany being united without revolution. The Soviets withdrew without great problems, and also the Gulf War. I mean this was a very active time, and it could have gone badly.

McCORMACK: Easily. We could also have had two German states. That is what some other European leaders wanted.

Q: And with the Soviets still glowering on the other side . . .

McCORMACK: It could have also triggered war or savage repression. But it didn't. Part of it had to do with the fact that the bad cop in this process was the previous administration, the one that put pressure on the Soviet Union, disrupted the war with Afghanistan, and organized the contras; all the heavy stuff. The Reagan people did the muscle work that was necessary.

President Bush was able then to play the good cop. That may be an exaggeration. During the second part of the Reagan administration, Reagan too softened his approach. But George Bush wasn't directly tainted by any of the earlier tough muscle business. Therefore the institutional elements of the Soviet Union didn't have the same visceral feeling of distrust, dislike, and anger toward him that they had for Ronald Reagan's administration.

Q: You were saying Baker did not have much respect for Nicholas Brady who was the Secretary of Treasury. Treasury sometimes is the antagonist of economic people at State. How did you find relations with Treasury?

McCORMACK: I never viewed Treasury's institutional perspective as a problem because a sound macroeconomic point of view is the basis for any long-term policy that is going to work. Secondly, it is important from an analytical point of view that the microeconomic issues are appropriately analyzed. In the first Reagan administration when I was the Assistant Secretary, we had regular meetings between the Assistant Secretary and the Under Secretary levels at Treasury and State once a month. We had no secrets from each other. That was Alan Wallace, Beryl Sprinkel, Mark Leland, and myself. It was a very effective way of doing things. This did not work quite in the same way in the Bush administration because the new Treasury team liked to play their cards close to the vest.

There is no reason fundamentally why the State Department and the Treasury Department should not be able to work closely together. We all work for the U.S. government. We should all basically value economic soundness in our policies. We all should appreciate the deepest insights we can get from our colleagues.

I personally liked Secretary Brady. I never had any problems with the man. I know that he and Baker did not get along well partly because they had both been on the Bush campaign trail in 1988. At that time, because of perceived differences of view, Baker supposedly forced Brady off the campaign plane. This relationship did not improve with time.

Q: My next question is of the White House or the White House staff. How did you find that during your time there from your perspective?

McCORMACK: It is important to recognize that in the U.S. executive branch, the President and his closest advisors drive the policy process. All the rest of us are advisors to this process, advisors to the President. If there is a constantly adversarial process between the White House and other parts of the executive branch, the latter are going to lose. So it is important if you want to be successful to be a team player. You need to make the best possible argument for the case that you believe in, but if the decision goes against you, you must implement the decision of the President or resign. What I deplore are people who will not give frank advice to the White House for fear it might damage their careers. The only damn reason you ought to be around is to offer the truth as you know it and to execute the ultimate decisions. One also has to recognize that the executive branch is a presidentially driven system. You can't have three people playing chess with one board. If you can't support the President's policies, you should promptly resign.

Q: You mention again how personalities and the person make something. I am not talking now about the President; I am talking about the staff. Sometimes the White House staff is almost personality driven too. Did you find that in the Bush administration economic-wise?

McCORMACK: No, I did not. In fact the people I dealt with in the White House in the Scowcroft-led NSC were wonderful people. I never had any problems with the White House. They knew they would get the truth from me. They also knew that I would never go out and leak. Therefore people treated me with confidence.

Q: Within the State Department, the economic business. How did you find this worked for you?

McCORMACK: Dealing with the officers in the Department?

Q: Yes. Were you finding people coming at you from different angles?

McCORMACK: Naturally the Regional Bureaus tried to get the most money and policy support for their region. The Economic Bureau was generally supportive of the Regional Bureaus on most issues but had a Treasury perspective and a bias toward orthodox macro and microeconomic policies as I did. From time to time, you had to make trade-offs between the political interests of a regional bureau and the broader economic interest.

The Reagan Administration tried to get strong economic officers actually working in the regional bureaus so that economic perspective was not an external consideration for them, but organically part of the internal process. I usually included regional economic officers in my staff meetings as valuable people to listen to.

Shultz was extremely concerned about the quality of economics in the State Department. He did what he could to increase training in the economic area. He, of course, was responsible for setting up the Foreign Service Institute and other training facilities at a big campus that he helped create. Shultz was an academic at heart, and many of his reforms continued after his departure.

Treasury continued to play its cards ever closer to its vest when Larry Summers arrived. This demoralized some of the State Department people who were dealing with economic issues, particularly those dealing with Yeltsin's Russia and the IMF issues that were involved. I personally believe it is a serious mistake for Treasury to play their cards too close to their vest on economic issues. None of us are universal geniuses. Economic issues are very complicated, and you are better off playing with your cards face up to your colleagues. There is less likely to be mistakes with an honest and open discussion of the policy process. Closed little cabals can sometimes produce big mistakes.

Q: How about internally within the State Department, during the Bush years, did you find any particular problems?

McCORMACK: Yes I did with the person who had my earlier job as Assistant Secretary in the Economics Bureau [EB]—Eugene McAllister. He used to take delight in humiliating his staff to the point that the Inspector General reproached him. Eventually, the Secretary threatened to dismiss him if he didn't clean up his act. But there is an institutional and inherent problem between the Under Secretary for Economics and the Assistant Secretary in EB. Both of them in theory report to the Secretary of State. In theory, the Assistant Secretary is supposed to report to the Under Secretary also, but he also has a direct line to the Secretary. It is the old business of serving two masters. When you deal with all the issues, you are inevitably going to have some disagreements. If you bring those disputes to the attention of the Secretary or the White House, it will create bad blood

Q: How did you work with the Under Secretary for Political Affairs? Would you get together before going to Baker, or did you both report separately and was there a real division?

McCORMACK: Bob Kimmitt, the Under Secretary of Political Affairs and I were friends. Bob was in favor of my coming to the State Department and spoke well of me to Baker when this was an issue. His staff might have liked to become more deeply involved in the Economic Summit process than I was comfortable with. Bob was, in fact, effectively engaged on the political side of the foreign policy issues. Bob is a gentleman. We had a good relationship.

Q: I mean did you find that you would get together to try to resolve an issue or weren't there issues to be resolved?

McCORMACK: There weren't very many issues to be resolved between us. I had the economic portfolio; he did the political work. He had the same kind of problems with Bob Zoellick that I did. When Zoellick left the Department, the new Secretary of State, Larry Eagleburger, abolished Zoellick's combined position as Counselor/Executive Secretary.

Q: Zoellick's position was what?

McCORMACK: He was the Counselor, and at the same time the Head of the Executive Secretariat. His strong views and management style were sometimes a nightmare for the rest of the Department. He was, however, useful to Baker, who knew when to seek a second opinion and who did not want to be blindsided by the bureaucracy.

Q: When you think back about your past public service, what are you proudest of?

McCORMACK: Serving as the sherpa for President Bush on two successful Economic Summits was an exciting responsibility. It was gratifying to see some of the strategies that I originated for addressing complex problems unfold with results. But there was one final contribution toward the end of my service as Under Secretary that impacted the lives of millions of people in a very direct way: correcting a blunder made by some senior people in the State Department that could have cost the lives of six million people in Sudan.

Let me explain what happened. In January of 1991, after I had announced my intention to step down as Under Secretary, I continued to attend the Secretary's morning staff meetings. At one such meeting, the Assistant Secretary for Africa informed the Secretary that there would be a serious famine in Sudan that summer because of a drought and locust plague that would impact both the north and south of Sudan. He explained that we had just been forced to close our Embassy there, which meant that the voluntary agencies, which were absolutely critical to distributing emergency food supplies, also had been forced to withdraw. So there would be no U.S. food relief.

The Assistant Secretary proposed to the Secretary that a public relations campaign be mounted so that "when pictures of all those stick figures" appeared in the media, wasted away by famine, people would understand that we had done everything possible. "We need to put a good face on the situation."

Baker looked at me, and I looked at him. Baker responded: "It is hard to put a good face on famine, isn't it?"

I offered to look into this situation.

It turned out that the Under Secretary for Management had ordered the withdrawal of the American ambassador and the closure of the U.S. embassy because of "threats of terrorism" to our diplomats.

Weeks went by and the Under Secretary refused to reverse his decision, claiming that the Department could be sued if our diplomats were killed.

It turned out that there were many people at lower levels of the State Department who were deeply unhappy with this decision, including the ambassador who had been withdrawn, but the Under Secretary refused to budge.

I continued to dig deeper into the matter, and discovered that estimates of deaths that would result from the famine this summer were in the order of six million people. I then made speeches about the impending famine in Sudan at Davos, the OECD in Paris, and in Japan to try to mobilize other governments to act.

I also looked into the highly classified intelligence reports that had been the trigger for the Under Secretary's original decision to close the embassy. What I learned was shocking to me. After reading these reports, I called a meeting with the Under Secretary of Management and other interested parties in the State Department. More than a dozen officials attended. Once again, the Under Secretary for Management cited his responsibilities to take firm action to protect our diplomats and to avoid a potential lawsuit.

Finally, I had heard enough, and I said the following: "I have looked into the intelligence reports on the threat to our embassy personnel that you cite. It was a rumor picked up by the Egyptians that possibly one person in the embassy was targeted for an attack. Because of this rumor and threat to a single individual, you ordered the closure of the entire embassy over the protest of the ambassador. This closure forced the withdrawal of the voluntary agencies that distribute emergency food shipments and terminated any U.S. ability to address this impending famine, thereby dooming six million human beings to death by starvation. I am leaving the State Department in a short time, but you will still be here, and you will have to explain this decision to the Congress of the United States when these people begin dying in their millions this summer. I am glad that I will not have to deliver that testimony, but you will."

Without a word, he leaped up from his chair and rushed out of the room. Within a matter of days, the Secretary of State ordered the return of the ambassador, and ordered an extraordinary emergency food relief effort to try to overcome the results of several lost months. Shortly thereafter, the White House announced that the Under Secretary for Management in the State Department would be taking other responsibilities elsewhere in the government.

The urgent emergency effort that followed was the United States government operating at its most creative best, and the famine was averted.

Later I reflected that if I had done nothing else in my thirty odd years in Washington, that single episode and saving those six million human beings would have justified my entire career. This accomplishment was cited in the Distinguished Service Medal, the Department's highest award, which Secretary Baker presented to me on my final day at the Department of State a few weeks later.

The ultimate credit for fixing this problem belongs, of course, to Secretary Baker. Dedicated people such as Alison Rosenberg, Jim Cheek, Andrew Natsios, and the able and selfless people serving in the Intelligence and Research Bureau all made vital contributions to this collective effort. Still, I know that without my particular contribution, we would have lost much more time, and probably lost the race against death that summer in Sudan.

Q: How do things like this happen?

McCORMACK: A similar issue arose in 1984, when famine struck many parts of East Africa again, with military conflict adding to natural disasters in some places to reduce food supplies. At that time, the governments of Ethiopia and Mozambique were both on the other side of the Cold War divide. Some in the administration favored helping those countries with governments that have good relations with Washington, while letting the people in countries under Marxist rule fend for themselves. Again, the lives of millions hung in the balance.

I remember seeing pictures of well-fed government soldiers patrolling camps of starving refugees in places like Mozambique. It was clear that the last food available in countries like that would go to those under arms supporting the despotic regimes. When the issue of whether to extend U.S. food assistance to the starving people in such countries arose, many of us took the position that the interests of humanity took precedence. We could sort out the politics with these governments after the millions of innocent civilians in jeopardy were rescued.

President Reagan did not hesitate to support our views on this issue. Famine relief and other food assistance were channeled to the stricken regions, regardless of political considerations. In October of 1984, I received a

Presidential letter of commendation for my personal involvement in this broader effort.

There will always be governments with whom we or our allies will have sharp differences of policy and interest and whose leadership we will have every reason to deplore. However, a famine created the circumstances in which leftist opposition with KGB support was able to topple the government of our ally Haile Selassie of Ethiopia. There will also always be a temptation by those, wishing to support their objectives, to let an unassisted famine destabilize unpopular governments.

America's past policy has been to address our political differences with the flawed government after dealing with the humanitarian crises. May this always be our nation's first priority.

NON-GOVERNMENTAL CAREER

Q: Then you left before the end of the Bush administration. You were mentioning ulcers; physically you really had to leave?

McCORMACK: After ten years in the State Department, one difficult assignment after another, and jet lag upon jet lag, I was simply exhausted. I didn't even want one of the low-stress ambassadorships that were offered to me. It took me nearly a year to fully recover.

Q: Are there any other issues or events you want to record?

McCORMACK: Yes, the Joint Economic Development Group (JEDG) working on the Israeli economy was a challenging part of my job as Under Secretary. Fortunately, I had the services of Dr. Herbert Stein to advise and support me in this effort. He was a truly remarkable man. Not only was Stein an advisor, but he was also a friend, whose friendship lasted until he passed away years later. This special joint group was originally set up to help stabilize the Israeli economy after the large inflation in Israel in the early 1980s, which nearly destroyed the banking system. Herb Stein was then the coordinator of that process under Shultz. When I became Under Secretary, I asked Stein to continue to work with me.

In the 1980s, the U.S. eventually wound up giving a billion dollars to Israel to try to get their finances back in shape after the train had jumped the rails. The JEDG tried to encourage sound economic policies while creating a better and more favorable economy and a climate for business and investment. As you know, Israel was founded by a group of idealistic socialists. There were all kinds of egalitarian processes built into the Israeli economy beginning with the kibbutz movement and the powerful labor unions. These processes constipated business and investment.

During this period, Jacob Frankel who was chief economist of the IMF, came to see me and said that he was being considered as the Head of the Bank of Israel. I appealed to him to do it. Frankel was one of the ablest economists I had worked with. There were elections coming up. Prime Minister Shamir naturally wanted to be re-elected. None of us, however, wanted a repeat of Menachem Begin's boom and bust.

When I left government in 1991, I went to the Woodrow Wilson Center and spent the next year writing papers on economic reforms for the Israeli economy. I delivered my reports to audiences in Israel and emphasized how important defeating inflation and promoting a successful peace process was to future investment and prosperity in Israel. These presentations received a great deal of local media attention.

When Frankel left many years later from the Bank of Israel, there was almost no inflation in the country, and the business climate had dramatically improved.

There were many other responsibilities of the Under Secretary for Economics during that era. This included traveling to key meetings concerning the Uruguay Round in Brussels. I also had to travel to Japan repeatedly to work on the Structural Impediments Initiative negotiations with the Japanese. In fact I was the first U.S. official to warn the Japanese in early 1989 that their financial system was in danger of collapsing. This happened after Federal Reserve Chairman Greenspan told me that I shouldn't be concerned about the Nikkei at 40,000 because there were hidden reserves in Japanese companies that fully justified the stock price at those stratospheric levels. I told him flatly that I disagreed with him and that I was going to move ahead on my assumption that the Japanese finances were in danger of imploding.

Q: You might explain who Greenspan was.

McCORMACK: Alan Greenspan was the Chairman of the Federal Reserve, and a free market economist. He was confused by the misinformation disseminated by Japanese authorities who were trying to build up foreign confidence in their overheated financial markets.

When I was the OAS Ambassador before I became the Under Secretary, Shultz had given me the full portfolio of material generated by our intelligence services that came into the Department every day. I had read enough of the intel to know that we were dealing with a Japanese economic patient that had cancer. Eventually during the course of the first meeting of the Structural Impediments Initiative that I chaired in June 1989, I said, "I have something I want to raise on a personal level." I then described my concerns about Japanese finances.

There was complete silence in the room. The only encouragement came from a well-placed friend in Switzerland. Six months later the Japanese financial system began its catastrophic implosion.

Q: Well you are pointing out something that often gets overlooked. Our intelligence services can give pretty good service for things that are happening, which you probably had better access to in the State Department than in the Treasury or somewhere else.

McCORMACK: Not so. Everybody with clearances has access to the same raw reports from our intelligence services. They are service institutions for the whole government. It was just a question of connecting all the dots and drawing the right conclusions.

Q: You left when?

McCORMACK: I left the State Department in April of 1991.

Q: Can you briefly describe what you have been doing since you left the State Department?

McCORMACK: As you know, I originally came into our system in 1966 and wanted to remain long enough so that I could gradually accumulate the wisdom needed to be ever more useful. That was one of the reasons why I never had any interest in press attention. In fact for years, I tended to avoid the press. My desire was to cultivate relationships of trust with people who actually made our decisions. What I have tried to do for 40 years was provide advice to people who have to make these decisions. I personally believe that the most rewarding life you can have is a life of service. In my case, this meant providing advice, analyses, and counsel. It was an ideal career for me.

I have worked for think tanks and various clients from the public and private sectors. Every year, I travel all over the world. I have access to top leaders in virtually every country. I have taken some major American companies such as Bell South, U.S. Shell, and others as clients. I spend the rest of my time working pro bono on policy issues that interest me. My reports and analyses are widely read at the upper levels of our system.

As new issues arise, I try to master the briefs. Every morning I rise at 5:30 and read five newspapers cover to cover for the next two hours. I have frequent meetings with friends in the government, and I travel constantly. The nice thing about not having operational responsibilities is that you can move from issue to issue. You also have time to think.

I will give you an example of what my schedule is like in the months ahead. On the first of June, I will be going to Moscow where I am part of an American delegation that is sponsored by a think tank. The delegation includes Woolsey, the former CIA director; Bill Schneider, the former Under Secretary of State; Jack Matlock, the former Ambassador to Moscow, and two or three other people like that. We are meeting with Alexander Besmertnik, the former Foreign Minister, Yakovlev, and four or five other top Russians. We spend three days a year in Moscow and three days a year in the Airlie House in Virginia, going through all the issues that separate the U.S. and Russia. Then when we return to the U.S., we send individual reports to policy people who are interested in these issues.

From there I am flying to Tehran where I am part of a delegation that will include Cardinal McCarrick, an important member of the U.S. Jewish community, and several other people. We will be meeting with the top leadership in Iran. Of course we are in contact with the State Department on these complex issues. From there I am flying to Austria where I am the Chairman of the U.S. branch of an informal organization that was set up 40 years ago to provide clear communications across the Atlantic. This organization includes retired senior officials from a number of governments of NATO countries. We meet three days a year in Europe, and three days a year here in the United States to discuss global affairs. Ted Shackley was previously the U.S. Chairman, the former Deputy CIA Director, and a very distinguished man. After this meeting, I will be returning home to the United States.

I have been asked to chair a meeting in Baghdad in July. I will probably do that. I have just returned from spending a week in Argentina where I had the opportunity of meeting the presidential candidates and their key advisors. As a result of these meetings, I wrote analyses of Argentine financial issues that went to the Managing Director of IMF, Under Secretary of State Al Larson, the Secretary of the Treasury, and other officials.

For me as a well-connected, independent analyst, it is almost a perfect professional life.

This profession, however, with its needful travel has added disproportionate burdens to my wife, Karen, a career employee at the Environmental Protection Agency. She has carried the major burden of raising our three children: Charlotte, Justin, and Elizabeth. I owe her a great deal; so do the beneficiaries of my labors.

Q: Thank you very much.

POST SCRIPT—AUGUST 2012

Following the conclusion of these interviews, ending in the Spring of 2003, I found myself at the heart of the events and policy struggles which eventually culminated in a shattering world-wide financial, banking, and economic crisis.

Initially my work occurred in Washington, D.C. in 2004-2006 at the Center for Strategic and International Studies (CSIS), where I wrote papers warning about unsustainable U.S. current account problems, a developing housing bubble, and related monetary policy concerns. My long paper on vulnerabilities in the global economy was included as the opening chapter in a book entitled *International Financial Architecture,* published by Palgrave Macmillan and edited by retired bank economist Carlos Palaez. The book appeared in March 2006, became a best seller in its category, selling for over a hundred dollars a copy, and was translated into other languages. However, perhaps because the book was a frontal attack on the Greenspan policy preferences, at a time when his prestige was at its height, to the best of my knowledge, the book was not reviewed in a single Major American newspaper. It sold by word of mouth.

In May 2006, I testified before the Senate Banking Committee in a session chaired by Senator Hagel on problems that concerned me in the derivatives sphere, and more broadly in the shadow banking system that was rapidly evolving. (See appendix I)

These writings and testimony came to the attention of the former President of the New York Federal Reserve Bank, William McDonough, who recommended me for a Vice Chairman position at Merrill Lynch in New York, where he too had recently become employed. My work with Merrill Lynch began in July 2006.

In the year that followed, I did my best to warn colleagues and clients that the housing bubble and the derivatives associated with it was a potentially toxic combination. Some of our clients, including T. Rowe Price's highly competent CEO, Jim Kennedy, listened and avoided the worst of the storm, which later broke over the housing and banking industries. Sadly, Merrill Lynch management, with a few notable exceptions, underestimated the dangers. These problems eventually led to the company's forced merger with Bank of America. I was one of the few survivors on the upper floor of the Merrill Lynch building, due largely to the able new CEO of Bank of America, Brian Moynihan, who was made aware by colleagues of the forceful warnings I had earlier delivered.

In January 2012, I resigned from Bank of America and returned to CSIS in Washington, D.C. to continue my research on the politics and economics of the global financial crisis.

We are now no more than half-way through this worldwide crisis. The timing and outcomes are not fully predicable because there are so many wild cards in this deck. They include oil-related geopolitical risks, the struggle to save the Euro, Japan's problems, China's unsustainable economic model, and all the strains that the necessary deleveraging at nearly every level of the global economy will eventually impose. There are also technical issues on Wall Street that require vigilant attention.

Much of the reserves of monetary and fiscal power that existed worldwide at the onset of the crisis in 2007 have been depleted in the necessary desperate effort to prevent a global depression

Thus, going forward, any new major setback to the global economy could confront policy makers with the temptation to resort to inflation, as happened in the 1970's, setting the stage for a subsequent round of instabilities and recessions.

It is important that great caution be exercised worldwide to lessen the risk of further disastrous shocks to the fragile global economy.

APPENDIX I

Listed below are a few examples of the hundreds of such policy papers I have written over the decades for our country's top political leadership.

1. "Some Thoughts for Newly Assigned Senior Political Appointees on the Management of Bureaucracy." The White House. June 20, 1970. (Woodrow Wilson International Center for Scholars 1992).

2. "The Twilight War." *Army Magazine*. January 1979.

3. "Obstacles to Investment and Economic Growth in Latin America." Current Policy No. 862. U.S. Department of State. 1986.

4. "Possible Strategies for Coping with the Japanese Financial Crisis." Presentation to the Association of Former Intelligence Officers. Washington, D.C. December 7, 1992.

5. "The Challenges and Opportunities in Africa." Presentation to The Center for the Study of the Presidency. November 9, 2000.

6. "Vulnerabilities in the Global Economy." *International Financial Architecture*. Peláez and Peláez. Palgrave Macmillan 2006.

7. "Potential Problems with Derivatives and Hedge Funds." Testimony before the Senate Banking Committee. May 16, 2006.

8. "The politics and Economics of the Global Financial Crisis." July 2, 2012. http:// http://csis.org/publications/browse?filter0=McCormack.

CPSIA information can be obtained
at www.ICGtesting.com
Printed in the USA
BVHW07s1927300718
523078BV00001B/14/P

9 781479 703746